Who in the World ?

Who in the World ?

Edited by
CLIFFORD CHRISTIANS
EARL J. SCHIPPER
WESLEY SMEDES

WILLIAM B. EERDMANS PUBLISHING COMPANY
Grand Rapids, Michigan

Copyright © 1972 by William B. Eerdmans Publishing Company
All rights reserved
Library of Congress Catalog Card Number: 75-184698
ISBN 0-8028-1435-2
Printed in the United States of America

First printing, February 1972
Second printing, May 1972

Foreword

Who in the World? is a result of the Body of Christ working together. What is written here comes from the spiritual and intellectual resources of the church. The book seeks to give a biblical portrait of the church and to describe in ordinary language what God desires His church to be.

The undergirding conviction of these chapters is that every local congregation must be an effective center for God's redeeming power in the world, and that the church can best put its enormous potential into action by having goals, by knowing who it is and exactly where it is going. Written for the lay church member, *Who in the World?* is designed as a resource material for Key '73, the North American movement of more than 100 denominations and religious groups that aims to confront every person in the United States and Canada with the gospel of Jesus Christ.

The book originated at a conference called by the Home Missions Board of the Christian Reformed Church. In August 1970 the Board brought together twenty-four clergymen and laymen to pray and talk together about the church's mission in the world. Throughout a week-long and demanding schedule the agenda was nothing other than an attempt to understand together what the Scriptures had to say about the nature of the church in the twentieth century. Months of careful planning and nearly two-dozen papers prepared beforehand by the participants provided the input for an extraordinarily fruitful week.

This book owes its life to the creative commitment to Christ and His church that brought these men from busy classrooms, offices, pulpits, core cities, campuses, and hospitals: Dan Bos,* Frank Breisch,* Cliff Christians,* James Daane,* Lester De Koster,* Roger Greenway,* Donald Griffioen,* Anthony Hoekema,* Dennis Hoekstra, David Holwerda,* Frank Kaeminck,* Simon Kistemaker,* Andrew Kuyvenhoven,* Earl Schipper,* Paul Schrotenboer, Lewis Smedes, Wesley Smedes,* George Stob,* Louis Tamminga,* Duane Vander Brug, William Vander Haak, Roger Van Harn,* Paul Veenstra,* Nick Wolterstorff.*

In addition to the conferees whose writing and discussion have provided the raw material for this book, a large number of other individuals and organizations have been helpful at every stage of the book's progress. The entire manuscript was finally revised by Lewis Smedes, Professor of Philosophy of Religion at Fuller Theological Seminary, in consultation with the editors. Special thanks are due to the Christian Reformed Board of Home Missions. Its uncommon vision for the church has inspired and supported the development of this book.

*These conferees presented papers covering the chapters and topics of the present book.

Table of Contents

PART TWO: The Life

Chapter Three: *Life Together*

Preface

Who in the World? The question is being asked of the church today by skeptics on the outside and believers on the inside. *Who in the world are you?* This book is meant to help the church, every congregation, answer that question for itself.

The book draws a portrait of the church of Jesus Christ as it appears in the pages of the Scriptures, in the hope that churches will compare themselves with this portrait and examine whether today's church *is* like the New Testament church. If it differs from the biblical picture, we must all ask how and why it does. Of course, the portrait that the book draws may have missed parts of the biblical picture, and it may not have pictured everything absolutely right. What is missing the readers in the churches will have to supply. What is inaccurate the readers will have to correct. The important thing is that we all make the comparison between ourselves and the New Testament church.

A word should be said about the arrangement of material in the book. The three parts are suggested by our Lord's statement: "I am the Way, the Truth, and the Life." The book takes Jesus' description of Himself as the key to the church's mission. The church must reflect Jesus Christ in the world; it must reflect the Savior in the *totality* of its own life and work. So our study is divided into these three parts: The Truth, The Life, and The Way. The church's mission is to proclaim the truth, to embody the life, and to follow the way—all as revealed in the person and ministry of Jesus Christ.

The concern of every chapter is the missionary task. In some senses, this book will not read like a book on missions, for it does not outline mission programs or give directions on missionary methods or try to goad the churches into missionary outreach. It does ask that all of us examine ourselves in the light of the Bible to see whether we are the kind of churches that are *prepared* and *able* to do Christ's mission in the world.

The accent here is on the positive. The book is not another brickbat thrown at the church by friendly critics. It does not add its voice to the chorus of critics whose only song is: "Something is wrong with the church." All it means to do is hold up the mirror of the Bible to the church.

May the Spirit of God use these pages to provide Christians with some clear hints of what our Lord Jesus wants His Body and Bride to be in these exciting times, and thus help His church—help *us*—be His faithful, free, mature, joyful, and loving servant until He comes.

PART ONE

The Truth

CHAPTER ONE

Mission and the Message

"No more words! What we want is action! Words only explain the world; action changes it. We have heard the words of politicians and the words of philosophers and the words of poets, but the world has not been moved by words. All the talkers of the world have left us where we are. Now is the time for doing!"

This is the mood of our time. Can the church go along with it? Or does the church still face the world with a word for that world? Shall we place the message further down on the church's agenda? Or, in the face of the activistic slogans, shall we keep coming with a message at the cutting edge of our mission?

The message at the cutting edge—this is our answer. The title of our first chapter reveals our stance: *mission and message* is our starting combination. The words "message" and "mission" both come from the Latin word meaning "send." So both words convey the notion of being sent out. The church is sent out to communicate a word; it is sent with a message. The message is the mission.

The church's job in the twentieth century is to proclaim a message. That—in the teeth of all the sentiment against words in our time—is the point of this chapter. We hope to make clear why the church has to keep to its mandate and proclaim the message.

A. THE CHURCH PROCLAIMS A MESSAGE.

The message is given priority in the church first of all because the church has a message to communicate. In other words, it knows something that others do not know, and it is charged with the task of letting others know about it. Yet this in itself would not put communicating the message first on the church's list of duties, for there are many things that people do not know which are not much worth knowing. But the message the church has is an absolutely urgent one, a matter of life and death. Not only does the church have a message that others *do not know,* but it is a message that others *need to know* with absolute urgency. Finally, what the church knows is something that the world cannot discover for itself. All the high-level conferences, the learned dialogues, the great books, will always fail to arrive at it. So we have a third reason for giving the message top priority: there is no other way for people to get to know it.

Let us look at each of these reasons a bit more closely.

1. IT HAS BEEN GIVEN A MESSAGE.

Basically, a message is a communication from some-body. It can be *news* about something that has happened or *instructions* for action or a *revelation* about someone. The church's message is all three. The Word that God wants told is news of what He has done, instructions about what He wants done, and a revelation of what He is.

First of all, then, the church has a message that *God wants told.* The church is not free to decide for itself whether or not it is a good idea to relay its message to others. The church was given the message for the purpose of telling it. God wants it known, and the church has a mandate from Him to let it be known. There is no way for the church to modify this mandate.

Second, the church was given the message as well as the mandate to tell it. The message, in other words, is not something the church thought up on its own. The church is a messenger, and a messenger always brings a word from somebody else. He cannot add his own thought to the message or change it or substitute another message. The church was *given* the message. This is all it has to tell and this is what it must tell.

So the church's message is always God's message, which the church only repeats. Its job in mission is not to tell the world what its brilliant theologians happen to be thinking these days or to engage the world's thinkers in dialogue or to share its insights into the world's problems. It may do these things on the side, if it has the time and occasion, but its main mission is to convey God's message.

Why did God send the church with a message instead of sending it with only healing, helping, reforming *action?* Granted that God did in fact give a message, a word, to convey and that He commissioned the church to convey it. The question is: why a word? The answer lies in the content of the message.

The message is about what God *did.* It is a word about an act of God that happened once upon a time in the past. God did something of utmost importance, and what He did must now be brought to the attention of all men of the present time. Furthermore, it is a message of what God *said.* Besides doing something, God spoke about Himself and His intention for men. He came to men of old, telling them His name and His will for them. He told the truth about Himself and about the world.

We shall not take time here to discuss *how* God talked, how He revealed Himself, for He did so in many different ways. What we want to emphasize is *that* He came and let men know who and what He is. Nor are we going to discuss whether God's acts or His speech came first. The point is that He spoke and acted together. His speech explained His acts; His acts accomplished what His Word promised.

Because God acted and spoke in the past, we have a message now. What God did in Israel's history and in Jesus was crucial and special, and our message brings it all into the present. What God said to men of old was also crucial. He gave the revelation then; our job now is to pass it on.

Another way of saying this is that Christianity is rooted in history. Happenings and communications that took place once, over a period of time, are completed. Since that time, the important thing has been to tell others what took place in the past. The church's job, then, is not to do again what God did once or to accomplish anew something that God showed us how to do. God did it, and it need not and cannot be done again. But it does have to be *told*, and this is why the church has a message.

2. ITS MESSAGE IS ABSOLUTELY URGENT.

We have said that the church has a message, given to it by God, about His words and acts in history. Now we must take a look at the urgency of conveying that message. We said earlier that it is *absolutely* urgent; in other words, it is not just an important message that takes its place alongside all other messages.

The message God has given the church is absolutely important because of its content. Paul's words sum up this content as well as any biblical text: "God was in Christ reconciling the world to himself."[1] The church's message concerns the life and death of the world. It is about what God did and said for the world; and what He did and said was for the world's salvation. If God had not said what He said and done what He did, the world would be forsaken, doomed, lost.

[1] II Corinthians 5:19

This message about what God said and did for the world's salvation is the *only* message about the *only* way of salvation. Jesus Christ is *the* Way. "There is no salvation in anyone else at all, for there is no other name under heaven granted to men, by which we may receive salvation."[2] This was the urgency felt by the earliest messengers. It was not conceit; it was not arrogance; it was not the pride of discovery that led them to make this unique claim. The message was *given* by God to men who were blind as moles in themselves, whose eyes had to be opened by a miracle of the Spirit. They were not the discoverers, they were not the originators of the message; they only bore witness to what God said and did.

It all centers on one happening in history. God had begun to act hundreds of generations earlier, long before Jesus came, but everything He said and did led up to what happened on a given morning in an ordinary garden. Jesus died and rose again. This is the event that makes all the difference in and for the world. This, Paul reminded his readers, was the message he had conveyed to them: "the gospel which you received, on which you have taken your stand, and which is now bringing you salvation . . . . I handed on to you the facts which had been imparted to me: that Christ died for our sins, in accordance with the Scriptures; that he was buried; that he was raised to life again on the third day, according to the Scriptures . . . ."[3]

God is *for* the world. He brings Himself to the world. This is what we confess when we call Jesus *Immanuel—* God with us! God lets the world know who and what He is, and He does for the world what needs to be done.

Now the world must hear, the world must believe, the world must obey, and the world must live in the new reality. And how can the world hear, unless there is a *message* given to someone to tell the world? But the world

[2]Acts 4:12   [3]I Corinthians 15:1, 3, 4

is made up of people. And people are faced with the decision of their lives when they hear. They can reject the message; they can call it nonsense; instead of being saved by it, they can be offended by it—as many have been. But they *must* hear. For it is a message that deals with their very being, their present and their eternal future.

3. NO ONE CAN DISCOVER THIS MESSAGE FOR HIMSELF.

The absolutely urgent message that the church has also receives top priority because no one can ever know it unless he hears it.

The church's message is not one that people may have thought up by themselves. It is not even a message that supplements or clarifies the best thoughts about the world. Nor does it merely put into words what people knew instinctively all along. At its core, the message is so surprising, so novel, so upsetting of what the wisest men had thought and said about the world and its gods, that it can only be called brand new. " 'Things beyond our seeing, things beyond our hearing, things beyond our imagining, all prepared by God for those who love him,' these it is that God has revealed to us through the Spirit."[4] It is a *revelation;* that is, it comes to us in a way that we could not possibly have uncovered by ourselves.

This message is brand new not just because of men's inability to think it through for themselves, but because men have willed, deep in their inner hearts, not to know it. They do not want to know God; "they have not seen fit to acknowledge God."[5] They choose not to know Him, and God lets them have their choice: "He has given them up to their own depraved reason."[6] So, we are not dealing here with an idea that men are ignorant of merely because no one has yet told them. They are *sinfully* ignorant.

[4]I Corinthians 2:9, 10   [5]Romans 1:28   [6]Romans 1:28

But now a new day has come. God has changed things. Now he "commands mankind, all men everywhere, to repent,"[7] "to repent and turn to God."[8] "It is not his will for any to be lost, but for all to come to repentance."[9] But men still cannot discover the message of the new day for themselves. This is why the church must tell it.

Let us sum up what has been said up to this point. The church has a message because God spoke and acted for man's salvation. It must tell this message because what God said and did is the only thing that could have been said and done for the salvation of men; what God said and did touches man's very being, his eternal destiny. It is, therefore, a message that man cannot do without. Finally, the church must tell its message because no one can find the message out for himself. This is why the message has priority in the church.

B. THE MESSAGE PROCLAIMED BY THE CHURCH IS GOOD NEWS.

Through the myriad voices that came to the men of Isaiah's time, one voice came to him and said "Cry." The prophet asked "What shall I cry?" The answer was: "good news."[1] What does it mean to refer to the message as good news? What is the good news?

1. THE CORE OF THE MESSAGE IS WHAT GOD DID FOR MAN IN CHRIST.

The news that we read in the daily paper is usually headlined. We can get an idea of what is happening in the world and nation and community by glancing at these headlines. Can the church's message be headlined in that way? Can it be recognized at the core as a single, whole, brief word that proclaims what has happened for man's

7Acts 17:30   8Acts 26:20   9II Peter 3:9   1Isaiah 40:6, 9

good? Obviously no one can tell the whole story in three minutes. The Bible is a long book, and the reader of the Bible needs help in understanding it (as did the Ethiopian in Acts 8). A preacher can speak for a half-hour, twice a Sunday, fifty-two Sundays a year, thirty or forty years of his lifetime, and not finish with the height and depth of what the message means. But is there a gist of it, a core?

Notice some of the ways the Bible talks about the message. It calls it "the good news of the kingdom of God,"[2] "the gospel of Christ,"[3] "the message of reconciliation."[4] All of these expressions have the air of good news about them. So if we are not to miss the point, we must express the core of the message in a way that conveys good news.

We can find an excellent statement of the core of the message in the writings of the Apostle Paul. He said that he preached only Christ. "I resolved that while I was with you I would think of nothing but Jesus Christ—Christ nailed to the cross."[5] This amplified his earlier statement: "we proclaim Christ—yes, Christ nailed to the cross."[6] Later he says that the good news he proclaimed was "that Christ died for our sins, in accordance with the scriptures; that he was buried; that he was raised to life on the third day, according to the scriptures . . . ."[7]

This is the good news at its core, in a nutshell. God acted in Christ to bring the world back to Him. God did something absolutely necessary for men, something without which they would still be prisoners of Satan, captive to the "law of sin and death."[8] "God was in Christ reconciling the world to himself."[9] God sent His Son, for love's sake, into a lost world, so that "everyone who has faith in him may not die but have eternal life. It was not to judge

[2]Luke 8:1 [3]Philippians 1:27 [4]II Corinthians 5:19
[5]I Corinthians 2:2 [6]I Corinthians 1:23 [7]I Corinthians 15:3, 4
[8]Romans 8:2 [9]II Corinthians 5:19

the world that God sent his Son into the world, but that through him the world might be saved."[10] That is the core, and it is very good news.

Everything else is measured by this. The church says much more than this, because the Bible says much more. But all that it has to add revolves around what God did in Christ for all men everywhere. If anything contradicts the good news, it is not the church's message. Even if an angel from heaven proclaims something different, it is not the good news; and if someone passes off anything other than good news as God's message, he should be cursed.[11]

2. THIS IS GOOD NEWS BECAUSE IT IS GOD'S NEWS.

The message that the church has is good news only because it is news about what God has said and done. If God had only told men how they ought to live or what was expected of them, it would have been bad news, not good news, for it would have been a message setting forth requirements that men could not meet. But the church's message is good news that points to something done for men that they could not do for themselves. It is very important for the church to keep the message clear and straight. If it changes the message into something like God's directions for men to comply with, it is no longer good news.

On the other hand, if God had only acted and not said anything, there would be no news at all. There would be, at the least, an event without a meaning, or, at the most, an event with a hundred different interpretations. It would be ambiguous, unclear, always in doubt. As it is, God acted decisively and interpreted His own acts for us.

10John 3:16, 17   11Galatians 1:8, 9

3. THE CHURCH'S MESSAGE IS A MESSAGE
OF GOOD NEWS ONLY.

The message of the church is God's good news. But is it not also bad news? Does it not have a dark side, like the moon? What about sin and judgment and hell? Are these not bad news? And does the church not preach sin and judgment and hell?

The answer to all these questions is No. There is only one message that God has for man—the good news, the gospel. The New Testament tells throughout of Jesus and His apostles proclaiming the good news; it never tells us that they preached bad news. There is only one Jesus Christ, one cross, one resurrection—and these spell victory.

But this does not mean that sin and hell are eliminated from our message, any more than a cure eliminates "disease" from a doctor's vocabulary or a victory and the end of a war eliminate "enemy" from the journalist's vocabulary. For the doctor or the journalist, the news is "cure" or "victory" over sickness or the enemy. So with the gospel. There *is* sin. There *is* judgment. There *is* hell. There *is* death. But the good news is victory over all of these.

When the church is commissioned to proclaim the gospel, it is meant to proclaim only the good news. When a man lives apart from the gospel, when a man rejects the gospel, he is left with all his sad, tragic, hopeless news. That is bad news, yet it is not really news at all. It is the same stale fact about life that has frustrated it and defeated it since the first bad news of man's fall reached the angels in heaven.

There is only one message, and it is good news. No wonder Paul was not ashamed of the gospel. Why be embarrassed at telling the greatest news ever? Nor need the church ever be timid. "You who bring Zion good news, up with you to the mountain-top; lift up your voice and shout, you who bring good news to Jerusalem."[12] *To the mountain top;* around the world via satellite. Preach it gladly. No grim-faced, joyless pessimist need apply. Anyone telling this message has to punctuate it with a Hallelujah!

Underscore it heavily. There is *one* message. And that one message is good news. It is a good thing to tell the world good news about the one thing that really matters.

C. THE GOOD NEWS OF GOD'S FREE GIFT IS NOT CHEAP GRACE.

Good news implies that something favorable has happened for us. The message is that God did something that we could not do for ourselves. God, who is gracious, saved us by His grace. "The grace of God has dawned upon the world with healing for all men."[1]

Now if snow is white, it cannot be black; if water is wet, it cannot be dry; if news is good, it cannot be bad. Similarly, if salvation is by grace, it cannot be by works. If it is free, it cannot be earned. If it is given away, it cannot be bought. Grace and works cancel each other out. "For it is by his grace you are saved, through trusting him; it is not your own doing. It is God's gift, not a reward for work done. There is nothing for anyone to boast of."[2]

Is the gospel then cheap? By no means. Grace was costly for God and it is costly for us. It is absolutely free, but it is not cheap.

1. GRACE WAS COSTLY FOR GOD.

God's grace cost Him His own Son. Nothing ever cost more. It cost His Son the agony of Calvary. Nothing on earth has ever cost as much. When we speak of the grace of

[12]Isaiah 40:9   [1]Titus 2:11   [2]Ephesians 2:8, 9

God, we are talking about God's free decision to pay an infinite price to bring salvation freely to us. There is nothing cheap about that kind of grace.

2. GRACE COMES TO CHRISTIANS WITH A PRICE TAG.

Grace comes to us, too, with a price tag of sorts. It comes freely, for the noblest of men could never earn it. But it comes freely with demands clearly written all over it. These demands are not in fine print, so they should catch no one by surprise. The implications of accepting free grace are very plain: "If anyone wishes to be a follower of mine, he must leave self behind; he must take up his cross and come with me."[3] It is clear from these words of Jesus that grace demands everything from us: our very selves as servants, totally given to Him. It comes down to this: everyone who accepts God's grace, His gift of freedom, becomes a servant for life. The rest of this book is an exploration of the demands of that grace.

Grace introduces men to a new way of life, the way of total obedience to the will of God. To talk about obedience to God's will reminds us of the law of God. Now, outside of grace this law is a heavy load, big enough to pin us down at every corner and to crush us. It offers no escape clauses or loopholes. Once exposed by it, we are condemned. Everyone who tries to make it by obeying the moral law is fighting a losing battle.

Saved by grace, we are free from the law. But we are free from it so that we can use it. Free from mastery by the law, we are given it to use as our guide. Though it seems strange to some people, Paul tells us that we are "no longer under the law,"[4] that we have "died to the law,"[5] so that "the commandment of the law may find fulfilment in us."[6] "For the grace of God has dawned upon the world

[3]Matthew 16:24   [4]Romans 6:14   [5]Galatians 2:19   [6]Romans 8:4

with healing for all mankind; and by it we are disciplined to renounce godless ways and worldly desires, and to live a life of temperance, honesty, and godliness in the present age."[7] The free grace of God comes with a demand and with a power. It comes asking all from us and enabling us to do all. Such grace is not cheap.

3. THIS COSTLY GRACE IS NOT PREACHED CHEAPLY.

This grace, which is costly for God and for us, is not preached cheaply. The church does not come to the world peddling Jesus or begging men to believe. It comes with the urgency of God's great news, the truth that He revealed and He gives. The gospel is not a commodity that man is free to take or leave according to his tastes. So the church comes, in love, with the urgency of truth, commanding men to believe. "As for the times of ignorance, God has overlooked them; but now he commands mankind, all men everywhere, to repent."[8]

We must be careful here. The church does not practice imperialism. It does not come proudly. It does not come with a sword, though it has been known foolishly to try that. It does not come with its own right to command. It comes only with God's command.

The church comes to men with a "joyful sound." It proclaims in faith that every man is obligated to believe what it proclaims because it is the truth of God. There is no playing on man's sympathies, no gimmicks, no apologies. The church comes with only the good news and the command to believe it and enter into the joy of it.

D. THE CHURCH PROCLAIMS ITS MESSAGE IN LANGUAGE THAT SPEAKS TODAY.

The church has one message, one gospel, but there are several perspectives on it. It proclaims one Christ, but

[7]Titus 2:11, 12   [8]Acts 17:30

there are different viewpoints from which to see Him. This is why the New Testament was written by more than one person. Each writer witnessed to the one Christ from his own special perspective in a way that spoke to his own special audience. The words used vary from witness to witness. Each writer tried to get his audience to understand the one gospel in their own language. Matthew would not have thought of calling God's Son the Word, as John did. But John's audience understood that. John, on the other hand, did not talk much about Jesus as the hope of Israel, as Matthew did constantly. The variations are many, but they are always variations on the one theme.

This has been true of the church's message through the centuries. The church has had to translate the gospel into many languages—a difficult task, as anyone who uses two languages knows first hand. It is fairly easy to find a word that almost fits, but much more difficult to give an exact equivalent. Yet no matter how difficult the task of translation is, it is a necessary one, for the job of the church is to disciple all the nations.

Not only is the language of one people different from the language of another: each language itself changes with the times. People who have read Shakespeare in school know how much the English language has changed in the last few centuries. What we notice less often is that language changes within a single generation—though this is surely obvious to anyone who is a parent of teen-agers.

Moreover, certain words are more prominent in some ages than they are in others. As great movements bid to revolutionize society, as needs are felt in new and powerful ways, some words come to the fore. The church in our time has an opportunity to translate the gospel in terms that are especially alive and prominent today. Let us look at some variations on the theme in terms of three words very much in the forefront of today's language.

1. THE GOSPEL IS A MESSAGE OF FREEDOM FOR MAN.

The magic word of this era is freedom. Name a cause, and the word "freedom" or a close equivalent is probably connected with it: "sexual freedom," "Gay Liberation," "the National Liberation Front," "free enterprise," "Free Speech Movement," "the free press," "women's liberation," and so on. The *word* "freedom" crops up everywhere because man thirsts for the reality of it. Even when the word is cheapened or misused as a slogan to disguise intolerance, its use betrays the deep longing of every human being for authentic freedom, and the elusiveness of its reality.

Is there a word that lies closer to the heart of the good news than this word? Jesus put the sign of freedom on His own ministry. True freedom was what it was all about. "If the Son sets you free, you will indeed be free."[1] "The Spirit of the Lord is on me, because ... he has sent me ... to proclaim release for prisoners ... , to let the broken victims go free."[2]

The church's message is a freedom cry. That must be made clear. But the church also has to make plain what the bondage in the background is. "Free," said Paul, "from the law of sin and death."[3] There is freedom *from* something: freedom from the frustrating chains of moral defeat, freedom from the despair unto death that besets the guilty man, freedom from the futile job of trying to satisfy God's demands on our own, freedom from the silly pretenses we all make when we think we stand on our own, freedom from the desperate need to make believe, freedom from our pious, moral masks, freedom from judgment at the end, freedom from fear of hell. Freedom *from*: this is the negative side of freedom.

This is an important side of freedom, because it tells people where real captivity is. But the church must make it

[1] John 8:36   [2] Luke 4:18   [3] Romans 8:2

utterly clear that freedom in Christ from all these forms of bondage is also freedom *for* something. A man can be freed from drudgery by a machine and then turn around and become a slave of that machine. A politically free society may be endowed with anxiety and bound by fears. A man free from poverty can be a prisoner of his abundance. Freedom from one thing often leads only to bondage to another. Freedom *from* is not enough.

Christ brings the basic human freedom—freedom *for*. He makes us free *for* being a neighbor to other men, free for being a genuine human being, free for living the life of the spirit, free for loving unbound by prejudice and suspicion, free for serving the Lord in whose service freedom is really discovered, free for growing into true manhood "measured by nothing less than the full stature of Christ,"[4] free for giving. Freedom to be new creatures in Christ: this is the positive side of freedom.

No wonder, then, that Paul is eager for Christians to preserve their freedom. "Christ set us free, to be free men."[5] The worst thing that can happen to a Christian person is for him to go back on the freedom Christ gave him. But it is almost as bad for him to shrink his freedom down to freedom *from*. "You, my friends, were called to be free men; only do not turn your freedom into license for your lower nature, but be servants to one another in love."[6]

The church in our time has a choice opportunity to ring out freedom to the captives of modernity. Its message exposes the deep roots of human bondage. It shows what happened when a man and a woman sought freedom from God. It tells what really happens when men and women become slaves to sin. But it reveals God's powerful gift of the Spirit of freedom, the Spirit who accompanies God's own free gift of grace. Man is on a treadmill calling out for

[4]Ephesians 4:13   [5]Galatians 5:1   [6]Galatians 5:13

liberation. The church has a message—a powerful message—of freedom for him.

One word of caution: the church that preaches freedom must be sure that it practices freedom. The church that brings the message of freedom had better demonstrate in its own life that its people are free indeed.

2. THE GOSPEL IS A MESSAGE OF RECONCILIATION.

One fitting word to characterize the modern world is "fractured." Brokenness is the plague of our time. Things that belong together are separated and cannot get together again. Another, more personally tragic word is "estrangement." People who belong together are separated. One marriage in four ends in estrangement. This is only a symptom of an epidemic inside of life. Call the disease segregation, and you get the division between races. Call it class war, and you get the clash between economic levels. Call it a generation gap, and you get the estrangement between ages. Call it sin, and you get the estrangement of man from his home with God.

Reconciliation means bringing together what has been broken, reuniting what has been divided. The root of estrangement is man's separation from his Creator; the solution is in what God has done for His people. "Formerly you were yourselves estranged from God: you were his enemies in heart and mind, and your deeds were evil. But now by Christ's death . . . God has reconciled you to himself."[7] Alienated, hostile, at odds, divided—but now reconciled. This is the message the church has been given.

There are many estrangements in life, but the one with the most tragic consequences is to be separated from God. The answer to it is what God did; and that is the message the church brings: "God was in Christ reconciling the

[7]Colossians 1:21, 22

world to himself."[8] And the word is out: since God has
reconciled the world—you—in your hostility and fear, *you*
"be reconciled to God."[9]

But there is another tragic estrangement that destroys
happiness in human life: estrangement between *people.*
Life is meant to be lived together. Human life has to be
shared to be human. Humanity really fails to be human as
long as walls of suspicion and hate divide us. None of us is
truly human until those walls are broken down and we
meet one another in love. This is what humanity longs for
in its better moments. It is what the "youth revolt" and
the "sensitivity group" fad are all about: people reaching
out, grasping for a bit of humanness in an inhuman world.

What better time to bring the message of reconciliation?
God's purpose is precisely this: to break down the dividing
walls between men,[10] to make the social and racial differences between them irrelevant to their union as men, to
make all men one in Christ. This is what Paul is talking
about. "There is no such thing as Jew and Greek, slave and
freeman, male and female; for you are all one person in
Christ Jesus."[11]

In Christ, we can stop being afraid of each other, stop
making a path to success through the ruins of other
people's lives, stop dividing the human race up according
to color, race, or status. In Christ, nothing matters but that
we are free to love and trust each other because we belong
to each other. No wonder, then, that Paul says that Christians together form one new body.[12]

The good news is that Christ dismantled the wall. Once
the wall was down, nobody had a special claim on God,
and nobody had a reason to stay apart from anyone else.
Now black and white meet on one, single platform: their
oneness in Christ. Young and old can work out their age

[8]II Corinthians 5:19   [9]II Corinthians 5:20   [10]Read Ephesians 2:12-16
[11]Galatians 3:28   [12]Read I Corinthians 12

gap within the circle of oneness in Christ. The message is for today: reconciliation to a fractured world.

One word of caution is in order. When the church preaches the message of reconciliation, it must also make sure that it is living the reconciled life together. It will be hard for a segregated church to preach the message of the broken-down wall, since it has built the wall up again.

3. THE GOSPEL IS A MESSAGE OF HOPE FOR THE WORLD.

People today have become future conscious. Magazines devoted to the future are eagerly read by government and business leaders. Books about the future are bestsellers. There are people called "futurists" who make a career of studying the future.

All of us are future conscious because the future is breaking in on us with terrible shock waves. Nowhere are people content to settle their roots in the past. If you talk wistfully about "the good old days," your younger listeners will not even understand you. The world has changed so dramatically and quickly that the childhood of a man sixty years old is like the dark ages to a boy of ten. What captivates people today is talk about the future and what it can or will bring.

Are people secure as they face the future? Or, as the title of a best-seller suggests, do they suffer from "future shock"? Being aware of the future is something different from being *hopeful* about it.

No one really dares to promise a *better* world in the future. It may be a more efficient world, a world with more gadgets to choose between. It may be a more leisurely world, though we will rush madly and work feverishly to enjoy the leisure. But it may also be a world so polluted and crowded that no human being will survive in it. Who knows? And what of that horrible thing which many of us have almost forgotten—the thermonuclear device, a soothing name for the doomsday bomb? Is there any real ground for hope as we rush into the future?

Fertile imaginations a century ago described a world of the future called *Utopia*. But Utopia is what the name itself means: *No-place*. To readers of modern fiction, the terrible prospects of Huxley's *Brave New World* or Orwell's *1984* seem more realistic than the beautiful visions conjured up in the previous century. The closer we get to the future the worse it looks.

The church's message to this situation is a message of *hope*. What of the future? The apostle says that we "look forward to new heavens and a new earth, the home of justice."[13] What is a Christian? He is a person who has been given "a new birth into a living hope."[14] What marks the person who has tasted the grace of God? He looks "forward to the happy fulfilment of our hope . . . ."[15] In the early days of Christianity, when the future looked hopeless to most people, the Christian was defined as a person with hope.

The whole Bible is future-oriented. From the days when Abram set out on his journey into God's future to the time when the Apostle John saw his vision of the future at Patmos, the Bible always pointed forward. Expectation, promise, hope—this is the mood. Many early Christians placed emblems of an anchor on their walls as a symbol of this. Hope "is like an anchor for our lives, an anchor safe and secure."[16]

But let us take a closer look at the surprising kind of hope that the church's message proclaims. Normally, when we say we "hope" for something, we mean that we wish for something that may or may not come true. We hope when we are not sure how things will turn out. If you are hoping, you are not certain. But the gospel turns hope

[13]II Peter 3:13   [14]I Peter 1:3   [15]Titus 2:13   [16]Hebrews 6:19

inside out. To the Christian hope is offered as a sure thing. This is why the Bible depicts hope as an "anchor safe and sure," not as a straw in the wind.

Christian hope means certainty. But it is still hope, and like all hope it cannot see what it hopes for. The Bible underscores this; if you could see it, hold it, claim it now, it would not be hope.[17] Hope is for the future, but it is for a *certain* future.

The only thing that makes our hope certain is what we have called the core of the church's message: the cross and resurrection of Jesus. We are made new men, born again to a living hope "by the resurrection of Jesus Christ from the dead."[18] Everything, including hope for the future, is tied up with God's new act in Christ. So our certainty, our hope, rests with the reality of Christ's resurrection. It all boils down to this: "if Christ was not raised, your faith has nothing in it,"[19] and so, too, we would have no hope. But—sing Hallelujah!—"the truth is, Christ was raised to life."[20]

What the gospel offers is not a self-centered dream for each individual that he will survive death. To be sure, life after death is part of it: nothing is worth anything without this. The gospel does point to a life of tearless joy, no more death, no more pain, no more destructiveness. But that is far from the whole of it. The church's message does not merely satisfy the survival instinct of every man. The church's message is hope for the *world*, the whole of it.

"We look forward to new heavens *and a new earth*, the home of justice."[21] Christianity is also earthly. God became flesh, and in becoming flesh He created the beginnings of a new earth. Great good news! The whole earth is going to join the Hallelujah to God the Creator, and men will dwell in brotherhood and peace.

[17] Read Romans 8:24   [18] I Peter 1:3   [19] I Corinthians 15:17
[20] I Corinthians 15:20   [21] II Peter 3:13

We do not call men to summon up *courage*, to grit their teeth and face the future bravely. We call them to receive the good news and to let the message change them, inside and out, into men of glad and confident hope. Nothing could conceivably be more relevant to the needs of our time than that message—that God was in Christ providing hope for a despairing world.

A word of caution, again. The church that dares to proclaim hope to the world must itself live by hope. Joyless courage in the face of uncertain disaster is not the mood of the church that preaches the message of hope. We must lift up your hearts, for our salvation is coming closer. We already have the down payment on the future. "God himself has shaped us for this very end; and as a pledge of it he has given us the Spirit."[22] So let no one proclaim this message with gloom, grimly walking to a threatening future. Let it be preached with head high, with calm expectation that all of God's promises will be fulfilled in Christ.

*   *   *

The theme of this chapter has been the *message*. It is the forward thrust of mission. We have a message for the world because God gave it to us. It is good news. And it is the one thing about the church's task in the world that is absolutely inexpendable. But the harder task is ahead. We have seen that the church's message was given to it, not discovered or thought up by it. The message was handed down. Now we must look more closely at the church itself. We must ask some difficult and persistent questions about *ourselves.* You and I—we are the church. Everything we will be asking about the church in the rest of this book will have to be answered personally. When we ask, "Is the church willing?" we are really asking "Am I willing?"

[22] II Corinthians 5:5

CHAPTER TWO

Mission and the Medium

When we talk about the *medium* for communicating the good news, we come face to face with a miracle. God can and does use the poor human equipment we offer Him to get His message across. How much reason, then, for us to make our channels of communication as workable as we can! Our best is never good enough, yet He uses it.

We know that the gospel of Christ is an offense to the natural mind. Our concern must be that the channels of communication that we provide for the gospel do not add needless *human* offense to it, for we can keep people from confronting the genuine offense of the gospel if we put our own offense in the way.

God entrusts His message to inadequate men. Men are not like tape recorders. When the message comes through them, it comes through their minds, their feelings, even their bodies. It is filtered through the whole human spirit. The human spirit can distort, disfigure, and disguise the message. But it can also convey it in beauty and power. All of us must take stock of ourselves, the church, as God's medium to the world, to see what kind of medium we are providing for the message entrusted to us.

A. THE CHURCH SERVES AS THE MEDIUM TO COMMUNICATE THE GOSPEL.

Before we talk about the means of communicating the good news, let us stress four considerations that must be constantly in our view if the task is to be meaningful. If we do not bear these things in mind, our communicating will be ineffectual, despairing, unenthusiastic, unfocused. We will be offering less than our best—and even our best is not good enough.

1. THIS COMMUNICATION IS A TASK GOD HAS GIVEN HIS CHURCH.

We must never forget that the job of communicating God's message belongs to the church. The spread of the gospel as recorded in the Book of Acts involved the work of the church, not of independent preachers. Paul always saw himself as an apostle within Christ's church, Christ's spokesman on earth. To sum up: the church must *speak*, taking care that what it says is indeed God's message; and it must be the *church* that speaks, not just you or I on our own, for "the church of the living God [is] the pillar and bulwark of the truth."[1]

2. THE SPIRIT WORKS MIRACLES THROUGH THE CHURCH COMMUNICATING THE GOSPEL.

For success in selling aspirin, everything depends on a catchy commercial; for success in getting votes, everything depends on the candidate's image. For selling pills or promoting men, the medium counts all the way. Compelling men to enter the Kingdom of God is different. The medium does not count for everything. Behind the scenes is another power, the strange power of the Spirit of Christ.

[1] I Timothy 3:15

We cannot say how the Spirit works. It is enough to know that He does. The same Spirit who inspired the biblical writers to set the message down in faithful human language can be trusted to make the human media work today. Somehow He tunes a mind to hear and a heart to obey what the messenger says. The basis for our confidence as we proclaim the gospel is that "no one can say 'Jesus is Lord!' except under the influence of the Holy Spirit."[2]

Although we cannot say how the Spirit works, we do know one thing about how He does *not* work. The Spirit does not work without men or without the Word. The Word is preached by real, ordinary men (even by Paul, who called himself "the chief of sinners"), and the Spirit works through these men. While this gives us confidence, it also challenges us, because men can stifle the Spirit. Of course, the Spirit can still make it work; He can do miracles with our empty hands. But we have no right to presume on such miracles. We must work diligently to make the human medium—ourselves—usable. Paul's challenge to Timothy comes to us too: "Try hard to show yourself worthy of God's approval, as a laborer who need not be ashamed; be straightforward in your proclamation of the truth."[3]

3. AN INNER URGING BY THE SPIRIT ENABLES THE CHURCH TO OBEY THE COMMAND TO COMMUNICATE.

Some information is best kept secret; other things can be mentioned or not—it does not matter much; still other news has to be told. The gospel fits into the last category. The church has no choice but to tell the good news. Because it is a matter of absolute importance, on which the eternal future of people rests, we are compelled to make known the great thing that God has done. It is good

[2]I Corinthians 12:3   [3]II Timothy 2:15

news *for* the world, and the church must broadcast it *to* the world.

But there is another compulsion here. Once the Spirit of Christ puts new life in us, He compels us—gently, but powerfully—to tell it. Something inside us pushes the good news to our lips. "The love of Christ leaves us no choice."[4] "I cannot help myself," Paul says, "it would be misery to me not to preach."[5] When Jesus sent His Spirit, He took care that His power would make the message work and that those who received the Spirit would make the message heard.

The church works under a mandate—the Lord's command to "go forth and make all nations my disciples ...and teach them ...."[6] He expects us to obey. But in the long run we do not do what He tells us simply because He commands it. His command matches the urging of the Spirit in us. The two are joined: We will to do what He commands, because He who commands gives us His Spirit.

4. COMMUNICATING THE GOSPEL AIMS AT CHANGING MEN'S LIVES.

The church does not share God's message merely to ease its conscience. To be sure, it is all to the good for the church to do its duty, but if we emphasize that side of it we can too easily excuse our shabby methods. What is wanted is results.

The desired results of the church's proclamation are lives changed by belief in God's message and obedience to it. God wants His Kingdom shared; and when the church communicates His message, He wants what happened at Pentecost to happen again. He wants people to do more than listen. He wants them to ask, "What are we to do?", and He wants the church to tell them plainly: "Repent and be baptized, every one of you, in the name of Jesus the

[4]II Corinthians 5:14   [5]I Corinthians 9:16   [6]Matthew 28:20

Messiah for the forgiveness of your sins."[7] And then he wants *many* to be saved and to be baptized.

God wants the whole message obeyed. He wants changed lives and changed communities. The message is not over once a soul is saved from sin. It does its work—its steady, powerful work—only when it pushes and pulls men's souls into complete obedience. Believers in Christ must become followers of Him in the world. The message is not only the announcement of Jesus the loving Savior, but also the summons of Jesus Christ the Lord.

B. THE CHURCH PREACHES: THE BACKBONE OF THE CHURCH IS THE PROCLAMATION OF THE WORD.

If we had to name one activity of the church as the most important, which would it be? The choice would be clear: *preaching*—the proclamation of the Word—is the backbone of the church. We hear a great deal of clamor for change in the church today, and among the ideas expressed, the suggestion is prominent that the church should attach less importance to preaching. Now surely there must be change in the church wherever and whenever the church will be the better for it. But to give up or shave down the proclamation of the Word is to paralyze the church and rob the world. The church and the world need not less, but better preaching.

Preaching has two components—the Word that is preached and the man who is preaching. We shall look at these in turn.

1. THE WORD THAT IS PREACHED ...

a. Is God's Word.

God's Word is the only thing that makes preaching worth listening to and the only thing that can make it

[7]Acts 2:38

effective. It is God's Word that the church and the world really need, not the preacher's opinions or an account of his pious experiences. The church and the world will get what is needful if the preacher will preach the Bible. He is a man, of course, and his voice is that of a man. But God's way to us is in humble form—the form of a servant. Our Lord's disciples were men, and He told them, "Whoever listens to you listens to me."[1] The same promise of Jesus applies to all who preach His Word.

We said that the church and the world do not need to hear the preacher's opinions. This includes theology, which is the word of man about God. Every church has its own tradition of theology, but no church should ever have to hear theology preached. Theology is not the good news; it is man's reflections about the good news. Let the preacher beware: his task in preaching is not to preach theology, but to preach the Word of God.

b. Is preached for today.

When God spoke to Moses, He used language that Moses and the Israelites understood. When He spoke through Jesus, He used the language that people of that day understood. God will speak to us in our language, too. This is why the Word is preached. If we needed to hear only what God said to Moses or through Jesus, we could get along with Bible reading and would not need preaching.

Preaching God's Word for today means that the Word must speak to *us*, in our time and to our own needs. The preacher's task is to translate the Word of the Bible into the Word for today. This means that preaching must be in our language. (That includes the language of our children, who have been forgotten in preaching for too long.) Our

[1] Luke 10:16

language means more than the language of our nationality; it is the language of our time and the language of our needs.

Preaching God's Word for today means letting God speak to our sinful condition. Sin is the same at the root no matter what the times are; but sin flowers in new species every season. God's Word must speak to the deeper motives of sin for all seasons. But it must also expose the concrete forms of sin in our time.

Translating the ancient Word into modern language is very difficult, and the preacher who does it well is rare. But every preacher must be given the time, the support, and the freedom to try. God's Word has a way of working when the preacher is free to let it speak.

c. Zeroes in on the whole of life.

The Word of God takes hold of souls and turns them about. To take hold of a human soul is to take hold of a life, and to take hold of a human life is to take hold of the whole of society. For a soul is a person, and a person is shaped and formed into what he is by many forces—his family, his job, his finances, his taxes, his pleasure, his politics, all his public functions.

This is why the Word must aim at the whole of life, not just a part of it. A man's religion is not a slice of his life that gets attention only on Sunday. A man who says Yes to God says "take all of me," and when God takes all of a man, He takes him in all his human relations.

God's Word must speak, therefore, to the sins and the needs of society. "Let justice roll on like a river and righteousness like an ever-flowing stream."[2] This is God's Word—not a comforting word to a private soul, but a gauntlet laid down to a people. All of God's Word zeroes

[2]Amos 5:24

in on the injustices that afflict the people—not of Israel, but of your town and mine. If a church does not hear this, it has no right to claim that it honors the Word of God and allows it to cut like a sharp sword through the sins and to the needs of our time.

2. THE ONE WHO PREACHES THE WORD . . .

a. Is a man.

The call to proclaim God's Word for today comes to ordinary men. The preacher is not an angel or a super-man. Despite the importance of the message he has, he says, with Paul, "we are no better than pots of earthen-ware to contain this treasure."[3] The preacher has days of only twenty-four hours. His understanding is limited and he faces real doubts about the deep things of God. His sins are the ordinary, earthy, sleazy sins of all men. Too often the church errs by acting as if it does not really dare to believe this of its preachers.

b. Is a man of God.

The preacher—this ordinary man with feet of clay—is a man of God because of the humanly impossible task God has given him. Poor man, that he should have so great a task! He should take himself with a sense of humor that *he* should be like "an apostle, not by human appointment or human commission, but by commission from Jesus Christ and from God the Father who raised him from the dead."[4] How can a puny, slightly ridiculous man ever be a man of God? Yet that is God's accommodating way of getting His message through.

Yes, it is a great honor to be a preacher. The office should be respected. But the preacher does well to forget

[3] II Corinthians 4:7   [4] Galatians 1:1

the respect and dignity most of the time and joyfully, with a sense of wonder, just be a man whom God allows to be a man of God.

c. Is a man of integrity.

The preacher must be *one, whole, undivided* man— this is what integrity means. He can fulfil this difficult assignment only with courage and with the help of his congregation.

First of all, the preacher must be one with the message. The truth must master his thoughts, his feelings, his life; otherwise he is a divided man. He must not wear a mask or play a role, no matter how great the temptation. The people expect him to be everything he preaches and to fulfil their ideal of what a man of God ought to be, and he surely wants to practice what he preaches. So he may be tempted to play the role of someone who actually *is* all of this. As time goes on, if he has yielded to this temptation, he may forget that he is playing a role. Then he has lost his integrity.

Another way that the preacher demonstrates his integrity with the message is by preaching its demands as faithfully as he preaches its promises. He consults the needs of his people; he does not yield to their prejudices. He determines, shapes, and grooms his message according to God's message.

The preacher must also have integrity with himself. His private life must be one with his public life. He should never feel the need to pretend. Consistency is the measure of integrity. In the pulpit or in the living room, the preacher is always his real self.

Integrity is a fine work of the Holy Spirit. It does not come naturally. The congregation, for its part, must never encourage their minister to wear a mask. They must let him be a mere man, even though he is a mere man of God.

C. THE CHURCH TEACHES: THE FUTURE OF THE CHURCH DEPENDS ON ITS IMPARTING THE KNOWLEDGE OF THE TRUTH THAT MAKES MEN FREE.

One of the important keys to success in the secular world is *information*. The future of the church, however, rests with *knowledge*—knowledge of the truth that makes men free. It follows, then, that the church is very much concerned with imparting that knowledge. It seeks to reach people by teaching them.

People today want action, the "highs" of feeling that "turn them on" to something. And let us be quick to affirm that the church ought to be a people in action, a people with feelings aflame. But first and foremost it ought to be a people who *know*. This is a time for the church to teach effectively.

1. TEACHING IS NECESSARY.

The church must teach because God gave *truth* in the gospel. The message we have been talking about is not like a modern, abstract painting, in which the purpose is only to evoke an experience—and what you *think* as you experience it does not matter much. To be sure, the gospel offers an experience, the greatest of all experiences, in fact: a new life. But there is more: the gospel comes with the truth. It comes to reveal who and what God is and who and what man is. There are true things and there are false things that can be said about God and man. The gospel tells us the truth, and that is why the church must teach.

Man needs to know this truth that God has given. The Bible thinks it is more important to know the truth than to feel a feeling. Without knowledge of God, without understanding, people perish. If one thing is painfully clear, it is the ignorance of modern man in the things of God. Man's great need is wisdom. So the church must teach the truth to man.

The church must teach God's truth to men who need it because that truth requires explaining. Though the core of the message is so simple that children can lay hold of it and know what philosophers seek to know in vain, there is more to the Word than the core. God's will is as large as life, and the writings of the Bible are as complex as life. Moreover, the Bible is an ancient book. God spoke to men of old, men living in another time and culture, speaking a language other than ours. So the Bible must be translated into a language that we can understand and apply to life in our times and places. God's truth is very rich and very deep. Its mines never run out. There is always more than we have dug in the past, so we keep on digging. It is possible to survive spiritually on the core of the message, but to grow into maturity, people must be taught and taught and taught some more. The Bible itself demands that it be interpreted.

Finally, the church must teach because that task is assigned specifically to it. The Bible makes it clear that the gift of teaching is entrusted to the Body of Christ: "some pastors and teachers, to equip God's people . . . ."[1] It is clear that teaching God's truth is not just anybody's private affair. "No one can interpret any prophecy of Scripture by himself."[2] Independent Bible teachers are a violation of God's method. The church is the teacher, just as God is the Revealer. When individuals on their own supplant the church in this role it may well be a sign that the church has failed in this calling.

Only as the church teaches will people understand; and only as they understand can they believe. Remember the story of Philip and the Ethiopian eunuch.[3] Philip, sent by the Spirit, came on a traveler reading the Bible. "Do you understand what you are reading?" asked Philip. "How can I understand unless someone will give me the clue?" an-

[1]Ephesians 4:11   [2]II Peter 1:20   [3]Read Acts 8:26-40

swered the eunuch. So Philip taught the meaning of the Scriptures, and only then did the eunuch really hear the good news of Jesus.

The point is clear. God gave us a truth that needs to be taught. People need to know that truth more than they need anything else in the world. The church is God's chosen teacher. So, whatever else the church must be and do, whatever changes it must make, whatever new adventures it must accept, this must not change: the church is God's teacher for the world.

2. THE CHURCH TEACHES A TRUTH FOR THE WHOLE MAN.

The truth that the church teaches is directed to the whole man. God's truth is not a collection of interesting ideas. When a man knows that truth he is not merely richer in information; he is a *new man*. The church must teach with this as its purpose—making people new. The church is not an information agency dispensing facts that will make people smarter than they were. Its goal as teacher is shaped by the kind of truth it teaches—life-changing, liberating, world-transforming truth. It is not feelings nor facts but the truth that makes men free. Why? Because the truth is *God*. When God reveals truth He is revealing *Himself*. Jesus said: "I am the way; I am the truth and I am life."[4] God—His love and His will, His mercy and His commands— is the truth we teach.

To know that truth is to obey it. Knowledge and obedience are married. All right understanding is born in obedience. If the church's teaching is only meant to make little theologians out of people, it is not teaching God's truth whole. God gave the truth in order to redeem the world. This must be our goal in teaching it.

[4] John 14:6

3. METHODS OF TEACHING MAY VARY,
BUT THEY MUST COMPEL PEOPLE TO LISTEN.

The Bible does not tell us exactly how to teach. But it is obvious that no one can be taught if he does not listen. If the teacher is to get him to listen, the teacher must speak his language. So the church as teacher must know not only the truth, but also know its listeners.

Jesus got people to listen by talking to them in parables, pictures of the kind of life people lived in that time. Paul taught people only as he became "everything in turn to men of every sort."[5] We may wish that people were different from what they are—that children could absorb spoken lessons as sponges soak up water and adults take in lengthy lessons on deep matters as our fathers were—but we must teach people, not as we wish they were, but as they are.

People of our time are tuned by the eye more than by the ear. In this TV generation pictures form the main diet; words are only snacks. If the church is going to teach the Word, it must first help people *see* the Word. God has given tools for teaching with pictures; the church must learn to use them. Business has learned how effective the TV commercial is as a sales force. Schools are adapting this medium for education. The church too must learn. As Jesus spoke with parables—word pictures—let preachers learn to speak with visible pictures. The entrance to truth today may have to be the eye.

A cautioning word is in order here. It is a shallow church that majors in technique to provide entrance, but fails to lead men further into the truth. The church must never exhaust itself in a constant search for teaching gimmicks while neglecting the truth to be taught. We must teach the TV generation, but our goal is to lead them far beyond the shallowness of TV. Every Christian ought to

[5] I Corinthians 9:22

leave childhood things behind and grow up into full maturity in Christ.[6] The picture can only lead to the Word; education does not end in illustrations. Christian growth in the truth means growth in thought and wisdom. And the church must lead us into grown-up understanding.

D. THE CHURCH WITNESSES: IT TELLS WHAT THE LORD IN HIS MERCY HAS DONE.

1. ALL CHRISTIANS ARE WITNESSES.

Not all Christians are teachers, but all are witnesses. A witness is a person willing and able to tell what he has seen and heard; a teacher explains the deeper meaning of the things seen and heard.

But although witnessing and teaching are not the same, there is overlapping between the two. Every true teacher is also a witness, for he cannot teach the truth of God without witnessing that he himself has seen and heard it. On the other hand, no witness can really tell that he has seen and heard something wonderful and important without telling *what* he has seen and heard. So, every witness is what we might call an elementary teacher.

All that a witness needs to do is tell what he knows. When the man with many demons was cured, he was sent back to his home town to be a witness. "Go home to your own folk," Jesus said, "and tell them what the Lord in his mercy has done for you."[1] It was that simple. He was not required to answer all kinds of deep and complicated questions. He did not need a degree from theological seminary. All he had to do was tell people what God had done for him through Jesus.

The first Christians were only people who had *seen* Jesus when He had risen from the dead. They could witness

6Read Ephesians 4:11-14   1Mark 5:19

because God had come in a real human being and they had encountered Him. They did not have to be philosophers; they needed only to see—really see—what God was in Christ. "Anyone who has seen me has seen the Father," said Jesus.[2] And the person who has seen Jesus can be a witness. This is the way God arranged it. Listen to the apostle: "It was there from the beginning; we have heard it; we have seen it with our own eyes; we looked upon it, and felt it with our hands; and it is of this we tell .... What we have seen and heard we declare to you."[3]

We live in another day. We do not see and touch and hear as John did, so we cannot be first-hand witnesses. But we can be second-hand witnesses, for we can tell what we have seen and experienced through the witness of John and the other witnesses. We can all tell what the Lord in His mercy has done for us.

2. CHRISTIAN WITNESSES SEEK TO BE EFFECTIVE.

Only a person who knows what God has done for him can witness to it. Only a person who has "seen" Jesus as Lord and Savior can witness to Him. The first qualification for Christian witnessing, then, is the individual's own experience of the mercy of God in Jesus Christ. And when he *has* seen Christ, he *will* witness. "We cannot possibly give up speaking of things we have seen and heard."[4] This is how Peter and John expressed the truth that one who has been a personal witness to God's love must tell others.

But there are other qualifications if one is to be an effective witness. The good Christian witness prays following a pattern set by the apostles.[5] Prayer opens us to the mysterious power of the Spirit, the presence of Christ, and turns us into effective witnesses, who not only tell what we know, but who tell it winningly.

[2]John 14:9   [3]1 John 1:1, 3   [4]Acts 4:20   [5]Read Acts 9:11; 13:3

A well-equipped witness also seeks to understand as much as he can, for he wants, not only to tell what God has done for him, but also to give reasons for the hope that is in him.[6] Paul did more than tell what he experienced and saw on the road to Damascus; he also "argued . . . quoting texts of Scripture which he expounded and applied."[7]

This must not be used as an excuse to avoid witnessing. The healed Gerasene was a witness even though he knew little more than that Jesus had done great things for him. But we may be sure that, once he became a witness, he wanted to equip himself more fully for that role. The calling to witness comes to us all, and we can begin as soon as we have seen God in action.

3. THE WITNESSING CHURCH SHARES ITS NEW LIFE IN CHRIST.

The Christian witnesses to people, not just so they will hear him talk, but in order to win them. "What we have seen and heard we declare to you, so that you and we together may share in a common life, that life which we share with the Father and his Son Jesus Christ."[8] The witnessing Christian wants to share with others what he has been given—a new life in Christ. Yes, he witnesses for the glory of God, but God is glorified when His gifts are shared with men.

There are three facets of this kind of witnessing to *people*—engagement, expectancy, and embrace.

a. It engages itself with people.

We must be engaged with the people to whom we witness. How can we witness to God's love for us if we show no love for people? The billboards that one sees

6Read I Peter 3:15   7Acts 17:2   8I John 1:3

along the highway proclaiming "Jesus Saves" can never be adequate substitutes for witnessing. God did not flash a sign from heaven; He came to us—*Immanuel*—and engaged in our living, our loneliness, our fears, our hunger, our death. This was the way of a loving God and of His "faithful witness"[9] Jesus, who involved Himself with us in order to witness to us.

Witness with involvement is a demand of love and the way of God. Churches who wonder why their witness does not win should ask themselves whether they are engaged with the people they are seeking. The kind of engagement needed does not happen when a tract is slipped into a man's hands. It happens only when a person gets involved with a man's life. It takes time. It takes sacrifice. It takes love. It takes listening as well as talking. It takes giving as well as speaking. A witness is a friend.

If the church seeks to witness to its community, it must be in and of and with that community, sharing its sorrows, seeking to heal its wounds, suffering its troubles. It must *act* to demonstrate its passion for men. It must be engaged with them.

b. It expects to win people over.

Churches often approach their mission without expectation. They do not expect to win because they do not dare believe it is possible, or perhaps because they do not really want to win people. Some try to pass this sort of defeatism off as "realism," instead of admitting what it really is—disbelief.

There are many causes for defeatism. One is the belief in some churches that God does not really want to save many. They pluck a text from the Bible that suggests few will be saved—and let that text set their mood. Defeatism

[9]Revelation 1:5

has a way of fulfilling itself. Expect nothing, get nothing. Believe nothing, receive nothing. Ask, expecting, and you shall receive.[10] God's promise is that "if you call to me I will answer you, and tell you great and mysterious things."[11] John describes his vision: "After this I looked and saw a vast throng, which no one could count, from every nation, of all tribes, peoples, and languages, standing in front of the throne and before the Lamb."[12] We must correct our defeatism by recalling what God told Isaiah: "So shall the word which comes from my mouth prevail; it shall not return to me fruitless without accomplishing my purpose or succeeding in the task I gave it."[13]

Expect? With promises like these, how can we not expect? There is a power at work in witnessing, a power not our own. How did your family become Christian? How did your church? Somewhere, sometime, someone came witnessing "to win over as many as possible."[14] If our mood is negative, if our witness carries a self-defeating tone, it will show, and the people to whom we witness will fulfil our negative expectations. But if we expect the Lord to do something through us, if we expect the Spirit to win men through us—even us, earthen vessels that we are—He will.

c. It embraces them into its fellowship.

Just as a family embraces a newly adopted child into its life, the family of God embraces a newly saved person into its life. A new Christian left on his own is an invitation to spiritual disaster. To become a Christian is to join the fellowship.

A new Christian needs a great deal of love. Embracing him can mean many things—getting his name on the roll of

10Read James 4:2 and Matthew 21:22   11Jeremiah 33:3
12Revelation 7:9   13Isaiah 55:11   14I Corinthians 9:19

the church, seeing to his transportation for Sunday service, placing him into a class for instruction. But what all these things center around is the fellowship of caring persons. To embrace someone into your fellowship means to bring him all the way inside, not just to share the sermon, but to share your life. Everything about him becomes the care of the church. To embrace him means to take him *as he is,* and to make everything that is yours his to share.

The Bible sets the tone. "We were as gentle with you as a nurse caring fondly for her children . . . . We dealt with you one by one, as a father deals with his children." [15] Later, we will be talking about life together in the spiritual community. The kind of life together typical of Christian community is the kind of life-giving embrace that protects and builds the new Christian.

God will have to forgive the church for its habit of abandoning its children. Many Christians are born into Christ but left outside the family of Christ. Or they are allowed in the vestibule of Sunday worship, but never embraced into the living room of everyday friendship. God's way is to nourish Christians within the whole life of the Christian fellowship. We must do it God's way.

* * *

When John the Baptist was in jail and began to wonder, he sent some of his friends to Jesus to find out just who He was. Jesus sent the friends back with this: "Go and tell John what you hear and see: the blind recover their sight, the lame walk, the lepers are made clean, the deaf hear, the dead are raised to life, the poor are hearing the good news." [1] Action and words—works of healing and words of good news—together! Matthew sums up the ministry of Jesus this way: "So Jesus went round all the towns . . . announcing the good news of the kingdom, and curing every

---

[15] I Thessalonians 2:7, 11   [1] Matthew 11:4, 5

kind of ailment and disease."[2] Again—action and words together.

It is hard even to think of Jesus without His acts of love. When the Kingdom comes in power, it does something wherever and for whomever something needs doing. It heals people, it visits people in prison, it gives thirsty people water, hungry people food, and naked people clothes to wear. It casts out the demons that make people go around hurting themselves. The Kingdom came in Jesus, and this is how it worked.

The Kingdom comes in Christ's Body. Does it still work this way? Churches that settle for *talk*—for the words of the good news only—are all too familiar. But from the time the early church first appointed the Seven to meet the needs of the Greek-speaking widows,[3] it organized for the right combination—acts and words.

The church does not have to postpone its action until it settles every argument about which acts are proper for it. Too often such arguments are only evasions of any action at all. There are poor to be cared for. There are oppressions suffered. There are sick to be healed. There are people, not far off, who do not eat enough. There are people in prison. There are crooked ways that need straightening out. There are demons that need to be cast out of human lives. Let the church begin where it is, and perhaps what the church does will speak so loud that more people will begin to hear what it says.

Technology has revolutionized everything. In God's providence, the church today is called to work during a technological revolution. The media are at the forefront. Business is eager to make full use of all of them. The church must not be on a side track, letting that revolution go by, unused for the greatest business of all.

[2]Matthew 9:35   [3]Read Acts 6:1-7

Films, some of them very poor, but now and then very good, are only one medium. Video cassettes are just around the corner. Pornography peddlers already have their plans for this medium; will the church be ready for it? Small portable tape recorders are used by many groups: why should not *every* member of the church be expected to own one—for teaching the Bible at home, to the children and to guests. Overhead projectors are useful in college lectures; can they be adapted for Sunday sermons? The revolution of communication through technology is only beginning. Will the church respond imaginatively? Will the church use it as God's gift to communicate the good news? God is ready. Are we?

PART TWO

The Life

CHAPTER THREE

Life Together

To begin let us look at two pictures: first of a contemporary man; second of a man who lived in Jesus' time.

The typical suburbanite is driving home, alone in his car. The windows are rolled up and the air-conditioner running. He is alone, in cool isolation. The radio is turned on: noise, but no communication. As he pulls up at a stop light, others cars stop alongside—more men, alone, in steel cells on wheels. Each sneaks a glance sideways at the others: a quick look, no communication. The light changes and he is off. He pulls up at his house. The man next door is in front of his house; he must be a neighbor, though the suburbanite hardly knows. A quick hello, no communication. He goes inside, grunts at his children watching TV, grunts a few words to his wife, and mixes a quick martini to get him through supper-time tensions. Supper over, he and his wife leave the children with a teen-ager from down the street and go off to a party where he drinks too much and talks too much. The next morning he suspects that he has made a fool of himself and wonders if somebody will use that against him somehow. He gets in his car and leaves for work, sneaking a sour glance at the strangers in the other cars along the way. He tells himself that the only way to get along in life is to keep your mouth and heart shut, and to hell with everybody else.

Jesus and His disciples came "into the country of the Gerasenes. As he stepped ashore, a man possessed by an unclean spirit came up to him from among the tombs where he had his dwelling. He could no longer be controlled; even chains were useless; he had often been fettered and chained up, but he had snapped his chains and broken the fetters. No one was strong enough to master him. And so, unceasingly, night and day, he would cry aloud among the tombs and on the hill-sides and cut himself with stones."[1]

Though these two portraits differ in many details, the message of the gospel to both situations is the same: Jesus dies to bring men out of the tombs. He arose and sent His Spirit to bring men out of their prison cells of aloneness into the freedom of life in communion. We who are in Christ are "no longer aliens . . . but fellow-citizens with God's people, members of God's household."[2] This is life in community. "All of us united with Christ, form one body, serving individually as limbs and organs to one another."[3]

Life in community was at the forefront in the earliest history of the church. "They met constantly to hear the apostles teach, and to share the common life, to break bread, and to pray . . . . All whose faith had drawn them together held everything in common: they would sell their property and possessions and make a general distribution as the need of each required."[4]

Our subject in this chapter is the spiritual community—life together shared with one another in Christ through the Spirit. Other chapters talk about what the church must say and do; this one talks about what the church must be. Other chapters speak of winning men; this one speaks of the new life in community that we win them for.

Redemption through Christ—being brought out of the

[1]Mark 5:1-5   [2]Ephesians 2:19   [3]Romans 12:5   [4]Acts 2:42, 44

tombs—means life together. Christ "has broken down the enmity which stood like a dividing wall,"[5] and has led us over the rubble to each other. In the church of Jesus Christ the prodigal finds a brother and the stranger finds a friend; persons find each other in spiritual community. The Spirit draws each of us to God, but as He draws me, He draws you—and so He draws us *together*.

Let us look at the spiritual community in three ways. First, we shall discuss the inner essence of the community, the community as God intends it, as it now is in deepest inner reality, and as it one day will be perfectly. Second, we shall talk about the outer reality of the community, the community as it actually is today, as people see it from the outside. Seen this way the community often contradicts its inner essence. Finally, we shall examine the community on the way from what it is today in practice toward what it is in essence.

A. GOD INTENDS THAT CHRISTIANS SHARE TOGETHER IN COMMUNITY.

1. AS CHRIST'S BODY, THE COMMUNITY SHARES LIFE.

The early followers of Christ met constantly "to share the common life,"[1] something that Paul urges them to continue: "Let your bearing towards one another arise out of your life in Christ Jesus."[2] The mystery of the life of the spiritual community is that it is created by the sharing of Christ's life.

The community is Christ's Body, as Paul makes clear.[3] We who follow Christ are limbs in His Body. Now what is it that makes a human body? What joins your foot and your shoulder? What unites your hand and your brain? It

[5]Ephesians 2:14   [1]Acts 2:42   [2]Philippians 2:5
[3]Read Romans 12:4, 5 and I Corinthians 12:12-31

is your life. This strange, mysterious thing called life surges through all your limbs. It ties all your limbs and organs together in one wonderful thing called your body. When you stub your toe, you hurt. When your head aches, you hurt. This is so because every part of your body is part of you, because every part of it shares your life.

Similarly, we as Christians are Christ's Body because His life surges through all of us, who are His limbs. His life ties all His people into the wonderful thing called His Body. "Christ lives in me."[4] Christ lives in you. Christ lives in all who are open to Him in faith. And with one life in us all—the one *new* life—we are one Body, Christ's Body.

Christ's Body is what the church is in essence. As such, it is the community of the Spirit. The Spirit brings life, Christ's life, in a quiet but powerful way. What He brings is the very power of the life of the Son of God. Notice how boldly Peter puts it: we may "come to share in the very being of God."[5]

This is the heart of communion in Christ. Usually, community refers to participation in something with someone else, but when we define Christian community, we change the "in something" to "in someone." We must see this very clearly. The spiritual community is not created by holding hands nor by singing songs nor by having meetings with inspirational speakers nor by enjoying a thousand potluck suppers. All of these may well be important demonstrations of that community, but it is created the only way any living reality is created—by the Spirit, breaking in with Christ's life. That is why we call the church the spiritual community—the community of the Spirit.

2. AS PEOPLE WHOSE LIVES ARE OPENED TO CHRIST, THE COMMUNITY SHARES FAITH.

People are united when they believe the same things. In the same way, Christians are a community because they

[4]Galatians 2:20   [5]II Peter 1:4

believe in and confess God and Him whom God sent.[6] In
the early days, we read, "all whose *faith* had drawn them
together"[7] gave up their claim on private property and
shared everything with everyone. Christians are one in the
Lord because they believe the same things.

But we would be selling this reality short if we looked at
faith only as a belief that certain things about God are
true. The devil too has "faith" in that limited sense, and he
is the crown prince of aloneness. The faith that binds the
spiritual community together is the opening of one's life to
Christ, so that "Christ may dwell in your hearts in love."[8]
"The only thing that counts is faith active in love."[9]

The spiritual community is a community of faith in
both senses of that word. If it were only a community of
those who believe that certain statements about God are
true, it would really be a group of dogmatic partisans. But
with faith active in love, it is a truly spiritual community
of persons who are open to one another because they are
open to the Christ in faith.

3. OUT OF ITS CHRIST-GIVEN RESOURCES, THE COMMUNITY SHARES LOVE.

"Love one another, as I have loved you."[10] If we
mean to take this commandment of Jesus seriously in the
spiritual community, we must look at how He does love
us. His love goes out from the power of riches to the
weakness of poverty, from fulness to need. It is a love that
arises not from His need for what we can give Him, but
from the wealth of what He can give us. In His love, He
comes to us as we are, lonely and hopeless sinners, gives us
what He has, the fulness of His love, and takes us just as
we are.

This is the love that creates and is reflected in the

[6]Read Romans 10:9-13   [7]Acts 2:44   [8]Ephesians 3:17
[9]Galatians 5:6   [10]John 15:12

spiritual community. We are not drawn together because we need the other person—although we do. We are drawn together because the other person needs us. If we love the other person for what he can give us, we stop loving him when we think he has nothing that we need. But if we love the other person just as he is, out of our Christ-given resources of love, we keep on loving, because our love is a *giving* kind of love. It goes out to the other—whoever, whatever, wherever he is. The odd characters—the disagreeable, the smug, the pious, the prigs, the proud, the dirty, the ugly, the stupid—are there also, concretely, to be loved not because we need them but because of the love of God in our hearts.

"As I have loved you . . . ." There are no strings attached to this love. It loves people as they are, in spite of what they are. It is a love born not of need but of abundance. Love born of need creates clubs—clubs organized to satisfy desires: political clubs, business clubs, bridge clubs. Love born of the overflow of God's rich Spirit creates a community of self-giving where persons are joined to persons by what each can give to the other out of the treasury of love.

4. AS FORGIVEN SINNERS, THE COMMUNITY SHARES FAILURES.

We sometimes call the spiritual community "the communion of saints." But saints are only sinners who know what they are and accept themselves as forgiven sinners.

All of us join the community at the same level. All of us confess with Paul that "Christ Jesus came into the world to save sinners; and among them I stand first."[11] But if we all stand first among sinners we are all equal to one another. This is why the self-righteous man never really shares in communion. He is always in a class by himself; he

[11] I Timothy 1:15

refuses to meet us on our sinful level; he is always above the rest of us. But in the spiritual community, holy masquerade is finished. The qualification for membership is the confession that we do not qualify for anything except mercy.

The spiritual community is a community of spiritual honesty. "Confess your sins to one another."[12] Why not? We admit at the start that we are guilty; why not, then, admit the real, concrete sins to each other? We are given the strength of love both to forgive and to accept forgiveness. So we bring our real sins and admit them to real people. We forgive each other, accept each other and help each other overcome. We cannot fellowship with one another as very good people because we are *not* very good people. If we try to create a pious community of good people, we only end up with an assembly of masked frauds—and this is not community.

5. RECOGNIZING EACH OTHER'S NEEDS, THE COMMUNITY SHARES BURDENS.

Life is burden bearing. There is no way around this. Everyone goes his way with a load inside. But life in Christ is burden *sharing.* In the spiritual community, as we said above, we share each other's life; and so, in the Spirit, no man bears his burden alone. We are all one Body: this is the inner reality.

This burden sharing is a two-way street. Sharing one life, we are as willing to accept help as to give it. Accepting help is difficult for us, because it requires us to admit that we need help. But through the power of love that comes when we share the life of the Spirit, we have power to admit our weakness and accept our brother's help.

My son is on drugs. . . . My wife is on the verge of a

12James 5:16

nervous breakdown. . . . I suspect that I am a failure at my job. . . . My arthritis is almost unbearable. . . . These are things that do not often feature in the pastoral prayer of our church services, but they are surely burdens. In the spiritual community, we assume that our "fellow limbs" want to share them with us—to hold us up in love.

Not all the burdens we share are burdens of the soul. The community is also a fellowship of the purse, a fellowship of labor. In the early days, the spiritual community saw to it that brothers were given jobs. An ancient Christian writing called the *Didache* (The Teaching) reflects this: "If any brother . . . has no trade, exercise your discretion in arranging for him to live among you as a Christian but not in idleness." In other words, the community does not only provide things, it provides work for the brother. One form of burden sharing is job sharing.

Burden sharing also means prayer together. The community does not leave its praying to the clergy. But real prayers demand real sharing. I share my burden with you so that you can share your burden with me, and we carry them together to our common burden-bearer, the Lord of our common life. When Paul told the community, "Help one another to carry these heavy loads,"[13] he was saying: Be what you are—the community of burden sharers.

We are burden sharers because we are a community of love. No false front of self-sufficiency! No phony strongmen need apply!

6. ACCEPTING EACH OTHER'S DIFFERENCES, THE COMMUNITY SHARES AS REAL PERSONS.

The church is a community of work, of projects, of doing. But it is first of all a community of persons. God's goal for man is to create a covenant community where real

[13]Galatians 6:2

persons are brought together in fellowship with the person of Christ.

But persons are complicated beings. The spiritual community joins us at the center, but even when we are locked together by love at the center, we carry with us all sorts of traits that make us the individuals that we are. We have differing jobs, differing tastes, differing talents. We come from different families. Our habits and our anxieties and our politics are not the same. When I share my center self with you in the spiritual community, I come with all my individual traits. You have to take me and love me as a *whole*. In love you accept me as I am, and I must accept you, completely, just as you are, a complicated person. The love that binds us together gets inside and works through to the center, but it does not demand that we stop being what we are as persons on the outside.

There is no communion of bare souls, no fellowship between naked spirits. There is communion only where love lets persons be real persons. The spiritual community lets persons be persons, just as God does. God does not kill individuality; He builds it within the community. This makes sense because, in fact, a person can be a real person only in communion with other persons. So, we can go a step further and say that the spiritual community does not only allow us to be persons, it *makes* us persons.

B. THE VISIBLE REALITY OF THE CHURCH FALLS SHORT OF THE IDEALS OF ITS INNER ESSENCE.

The actual congregation, your church or my church, does not always match completely this inner essence of spiritual community that we have been discussing. Now and then, here and there, it does look like the spiritual community. But its outward life just as often contradicts communion. The local church still has to become in earthly fact what it is in spiritual essence. This is why Paul on the one hand tells the church that it *is* the Body of Christ and on the other hand tells it to begin acting like it. The inner presence of the Spirit must become the visible power of the Spirit in real life.

Let us compare the visible reality—the church we see—with the inner essence. We will use the same list of qualities—only this time we will *ask* how the visible church compares.

1. THE COMMUNITY OFTEN SUBSTITUTES ORGANIZATION FOR LIFE.

The church is an organization. It needs order; and so it needs consistories and committees, rules and regulations, leaders and followers. Christ's community of life needs to do its business efficiently, and it could not last long without being organized. Such organization is not the enemy of life-sharing. Paul points out that it is the *Spirit* who gives this organization by giving gifts that, when used, take the form of offices. "These were his gifts: some to be apostles, some prophets, some evangelists, some pastors and teachers . . . ."[1] (We shall talk more about this Spirit-given organization in Chapter Five.)

But organization often seems to be the furthest thing from a gift of the Spirit. The organization becomes so well oiled that the community scarcely recalls what it really is: a mysterious body of people joined, not by efficient machinery, but by the surging, pulsating stream of Spirit-life. Would a stranger feel anything of this inner reality at the typical annual meeting of your church or my church? Have we lost the sense that organization is only a convenience to let *life* be channeled? Is there a waiting—a patient, prayerful, quiet waiting—on the Spirit who gives the life? Do people get a chance to face each other, touch each other,

[1] Ephesians 4:11

talk to each other? Is there any way to provide a sense that it is the life that we share which is our strength?

When churches do not really share life and no longer trust their very existence as churches to the shared life, they organize to promote the organization. What does your congregation want most? To keep things running efficiently? To keep the machinery moving? To preserve the organization? If this seems to be the case, ask yourself whether your congregation really does believe that the one thing that makes it a church is the reality of life that Christ gives to share.

2. MEMBERS DIFFER IN BELIEFS AND UNITE FOR REASONS OTHER THAN FAITH.

Look at the church around the world. It is not one body of shared faith, but many bodies with many faiths. The disunity that broke Paul's heart when he saw it in Corinth has become commonplace. We accept it as normal. But Paul pleaded with those early believers: "My brothers, in the name of our Lord Jesus Christ: agree among yourselves, and avoid divisions; be firmly joined in unity of mind and thought."[2] We cannot consider that the church is a sharing of faith without weeping at the broken body of the church. We cannot accept a broken body as normal.

Churches are divided by many things. Many of the serious divisions are caused by differences in belief. Sometimes, to be sure, divisions are caused because some segments of the church accept and teach a gospel other than the gospel of our Lord, but more often, the splits develop out of differences of opinion aggravated by human pride and stubborn wills.

We cannot even think about the sharing of faith without crying for the broken body. Can we pray for power to

[2] I Corinthians 1:10

perform Christ's mission to the world without praying for power to restore a unity of faith? Can we pursue mission without pursuing fellowship with divided brothers?

But the church falls short not only because it is divided by its faiths, but also because it is united by things other than faith. Often the unity of the church is only the unity of middle-class people, or the unity of white people or of black people. It is a unity of people who respect one another's views on politics or who share a common national tradition, a unity that can be called sociological or ethnic. Is it also a unity created by a sharing of faith?

Let us recall what faith is. Faith is surely a belief that certain things are true. But faith is more: it is the life of a man opened up to Jesus Christ. It is a matter of the open heart as well as of the convinced mind.

Sometimes a church is held together only by the faith it confesses with its mind. When church life is marked by a zeal for joyless debate, it has limited faith to a matter of the head. When discussion between members of a church demonstrates little grace and charity and respect and patience for people, that church is living off the top of its head. One-track crusades for right dogma, with little joy in shared faith, betray a church that has lost the gift of living by a shared faith.

If we are to share faith, we have to share one another. Otherwise we will only be sharing thoughts about the faith, and there is a vast difference between the two. If we can only tell each other about the doctrine of justification, and not about our joy in being justified, we are not sharing faith. We are not saved by right thoughts about justification; we are justified by faith in the Lord Jesus. The church's inner essence is the sharing of faith. Is it plain for all to see that your congregation is held together by sharing the faith that comes from the bottom of the heart as well as the top of the head?

3. THERE IS MORE TALK ABOUT LOVE
THAN DEMONSTRATION OF IT.

Your local church and my local church are often not communities of God's love. They are instead groups of people who live, not out of the power of God's love, but out of the weakness of their own need. We do not live out of inner strength, which goes out toward others just because they are there to be loved, but out of weakness, which goes out toward others with demands that *they* satisfy *our* needs. We make many demands of the community. When we demand to get all the blessings that we need, we are going out from weakness. When we demand that people in the community satisfy us, we are going out from weakness. When we demand that other people be *our* kind of people—nice, intelligent people *like us*—as a condition for fellowship, we are going out from weakness. And in all of these cases we are not going out from the power of God's love shed abroad within our heart.

The church of tense, pious people who want only "their own kind" in their community has missed being the community of love. The group based on likeness, on congeniality, on similar habits and familiar customs, is not a community of shared love. The church that cannot embrace the odd or different person, the nonconformist, does not move on the power of God's love within. The church that is not able to embrace black people (not just one "nice" black family, but several black families regardless of whether they are "our kind of people") moves from weakness. The church that impresses its neighbors only with its wealth or its efficiency or its religiosity or its size or its success has lost the power of God's love within. That kind of church talks about love and promises love, but it cannot deliver love to anybody at all, for it is not a community of shared love.

4. THE COMMUNITY IS NOT REALLY
A FELLOWSHIP OF SINNERS.

Our local congregations are *gatherings* of sinners, but they are not *communities* of sinners. The people there are in fact sinners, but they do not fellowship as sinners. They fellowship as pious people. Everyone in the community admits that he is a sinner, but who dares to act on that admission and confess his sins? A cover-all confession is made for the people from the pulpit—a blanket of pardon spread over all the people. But how often is there a chance for a sinner to admit concrete sins to his fellow sinners? The local church seems not to believe that James really meant what he said when he told us: "Confess your sins one to another."[3]

How can we ever be a community of sinners if none of us ever lets himself be forgiven by the community? How can we ever be a community of sinners when no one gives us a chance to forgive him? How can we ever be a community of sinners when the one thing we cannot allow is the candid mention of specific sins?

Sunday after Sunday, year in and year out, the congregation is reminded that its sins are woefully great. But does it really believe that? What if a just-converted prostitute, not quite straightened out yet, were to enter the congregation? What if a young black man with a natural hairdo, leather jacket, and tight pants, beaded to his hips, were to come confessing that "Jesus is Lord," and ask to join the young people's society? What if a parolee from the state prison, pale, shifty-eyed, insecure, were to shuffle into the communion? Would there be subtle signs that the community thinks itself more than a shade superior to these? Would it be apparent that we believe ourselves to be a community in which each of us is the "chief of sinners"?

[3] James 5:16

5. THERE IS LITTLE SHARING OF REAL BURDENS.

The churches where you and I are members are con-gregations of people who insist on bearing their own bur-dens.

To get your burden to the congregation, it seems, you have to be admitted to a hospital. The pastor always prays aloud that you will recover from your appendectomy. But the mother who is worried witless about a rebellious teen-age daughter goes it alone. The father who is struggling to make contact with his turned-off son goes it alone. The wife who is having a terrible time coping with menopause goes it alone. The man and woman who are in a miserable sexual impasse go it alone. Ninety-nine percent of our hurts are carried alone. We do not dare trust the Spirit to transform the church into a real community of burden sharers.

Burden sharing is work sharing too. If a man is suddenly out of a job, he knows where to go. He applies for welfare benefits and then turns to an employment agency to look for a new job. But it seldom occurs to him to go to his community of burden sharers. Too often, the last place a poor man wants to go for help is to his church.

This does not mean to say that no one in our communi-ties ever shares another's burden. But our communities are not regularly marked by burden-sharing life. We do not act together as if we really believed that anyone's burden is everyone's burden and that any burden of any man is the burden of all.

6. PERSONS DO NOT FEEL FREE
TO BE WHAT THEY REALLY ARE.

There may be places where persons feel free to be what they really are, but our churches are not such places. The church expects its members to fit, not only biblical patterns, but churchly made molds. The unwritten rules of church conformity often have more influence than the biblical ones. Congregations have molds to which everyone is expected to fit.

The community may accept a person at the center, but it is not always ready to accept the whole person. It is willing to accept him as a soul, but it has reservations about the rough edges of his individuality. What is more, few of us really trust the community to accept us as whole persons. And so we keep the community from being a community of whole persons because we do not dare take off our own masks. The community falls short because we do not trust it enough to be our real selves in it.

C. THINGS THAT DIVIDE MUST BE OVERCOME BY THE CHURCH ON THE WAY TO SHARING FELLOWSHIP.

1. GAPS IN THE CHURCH MUST BE BRIDGED.

The outer reality of the community falls short of the inner essence at each of the six points we mentioned. When it fails to be a sharing community, gaps develop. Some of these have been around as long as the church has; others break open, new, in each generation. If we do not try to build new bridges over new gaps, the community will be that much harder to sustain. Let us look at a few gaps that are apparent in the church today.

a. The generation gap is more than a matter of age difference.

The generation gap is first of all a gap of the mind and spirit. These days there are three separate "generations" in the church: we might call them the Ark Generation, the Exodus Generation, and the Rock Generation.

The Ark stands for safety in the flood. You are a member of the Ark Generation if you think of the church primarily as a refuge against a sinful and threatening world. If you do think this way, you want, above all, the Ark to be seaworthy and sound. The most important task for the church, in your eyes, is to keep it "safe and secure from all alarm."

The Exodus stands for leaving familiar places for strange territories and new adventures of service. You belong to the Exodus Generation if you think of the church first of all as movement from the walls of safety into the world of danger, in order to be of service there to the lost and hurt of the world. Your motto is not "safety first" but "service first." You are not as interested in keeping the church secure as in keeping it flexible, not as concerned with keeping it afloat as with keeping it moving. You may look dangerous to the Ark Generation, and the Ark Generation may look to you like a group of anchor-draggers.

Rock stands for being "turned on" *now*. If you want to experience the full power of the Spirit in your life now, you belong to the Rock Generation. You want to express your feelings, you want to be involved now, you want the spiritual power to be alive in you, with shivering reality, now. Rock music is a symptom of a need that people feel to experience some sort of inner clout now. In the spiritual community, this need expresses itself in a demand to let the Spirit take over now.

The spiritual community needs all three generations. But unless it builds bridges of love over the gaps between them it will not be a real community.

b. The technology gap makes us ignorant of fellow members' specific needs.

In earlier days, when things were less complex, everybody understood a lot about everybody else's job. Today a member of the spiritual community may spend much of his time doing a job that no one else in the spiritual community even understands. As a result, we can hardly feel the problems that our fellow Christian faces in his work; and we can hardly comprehend the problems he has trying to do his work as a Christian. How can we help him when there is so much about his life that we don't even understand? Yet in precisely this part of a person's life he needs Christian community. It will take a great deal of bridge building to get across these gaps.

c. The space gap separates people from one another.

Once the spiritual community lived together all week long. Our children played and fought together during the week and met at Sunday School on the Lord's Day. We bought groceries from one of the deacons. We had our cars fixed at a garage owned by one of the elders. The beauty shop where the women of the church went was operated by the soprano in the choir. We saw each other and worked with each other and knew all about each other, because we lived together in a real parish town. Today suburban spread has separated us from one another. We may see more of our gas station attendant than we do of the other limbs of our Body. We travel the freeways to get to church on Sunday, and when the benediction is spoken, we get in our private cars and speed back to our private places, leaving the community behind. But the spiritual community cannot survive unless it finds bridges to cross the space gap.

2. POSSIBILITIES FOR IMPROVING FELLOWSHIP MUST BE EXPLORED.

It is evident that the church is still on the way to becoming in earthly reality what it is in spiritual essence. The inner presence of the Christ-life must work its way out into the visible reality of your church and mine. The split between its earthly reality and its inner essence is never wholly healed on earth. Here and there, now and then, it is a real sharing community, but it has to keep working at it. The secret of progress is the power of the Spirit. The way of progress is to open the door of the outer life to the source of the inner power. Let us examine some things that may help open that door.

a. The sermon should be a communion-creator.

Some people think the sermon is a barrier instead of a bridge. Superficially, they seem to have a point. The main meeting of the community—the preaching service—seems to deny community. We meet as an audience, never looking at each other. What we see of most people are their shoulders and the backs of their heads. The sermon seems to create less communion among those listening to it than a football game does among those watching it.

But this is superficial. Sermons *are* communion-creators. The Word of God is God's way to get to us—to seize us with the power of the Christ who is proclaimed. In the sermon the Word is given its opportunity to grab hold of us together and bring about a real sharing of faith and life. Through the Word and the sacrament the Lord works Himself into us, making us one at the root of life. So, one way to build up the community is to keep the power on, and the power comes from God through His Word.

Does it really work? If not, why not? Is something perhaps lacking in the *way* the Word is preached? If so, what is missing?

b. Time is needed for practicing communion.

We tend to be prisoners of the clock. Our Sunday services must always begin on schedule, and if they do not end on schedule as well, the preacher is certain to hear about it. But we cannot practice communion by the clock. For one thing, we have to learn how to practice communion, and that learning takes time. Few of us really know how to communicate honestly and helpfully with others. We are so used to thinking of church business in terms of listening to speakers that we have never learned to open up to each other. And where we have a chance to talk, what we say is not *our* talk, but what we think we ought to say at church meetings. What would people say in discussions at church meetings if they really dared—if they really had the faith—to open up as real people?

For most of us communion in practice is a hard lesson to learn, and one that takes time. It cannot be scheduled to happen between ten and eleven o'clock. It is a long night's journey into honesty.

c. Households of faith can provide communion within the community.

Here is a biblical idea that has practical possibilities today. Divide the congregation into households of faith and life. Take five families at random (not five families who are close friends anyway) and ask them to get together at least twice a month. What they do when they meet is not the first consideration; the important thing is that they meet regularly and frequently. But they should not be called households just because they meet in houses. Each family must commit itself to sharing and bearing the burdens of the others of the household, to talking honestly about themselves and about the others—not just how they think they ought to feel, but how they really do feel—as in ordinary households. The households must agree to stay together for at least a year. They should keep coming together even when things are not working out well—and they should talk honestly about what is not working well. The important thing at first is to keep at it.

d. The church must pray together.

The shared life is created by the Word, fed by the sacrament, and sustained by prayer. But we must pray *with each other* for each other. The households provide excellent opportunities for this. It is not enough to mention an ailment of one of my brothers in my private prayers only. I must pray for it with him. Nor should we limit this kind of prayer to bodily things. The real test comes when you pray *with me* that I may become a better listener, a more sympathetic, less critical person.

e. The sacrament may be celebrated in a way that provides more fellowship.

Listening to sermons while looking at each other's backs is one thing; taking communion without looking at each other is something else. Can we break with the tradition of passing the elements of the sacrament through the pews? We might do this by serving communion twice every Sunday in small circles. Perhaps this could take place in the church fellowship hall (communion in a fellowship hall sounds right). Let a loaf of bread be passed around the circle, each person breaking off a piece. (There is nothing sacred about the neat cubes of crustless bread to which we are accustomed.) Let a cup be passed around, each person taking a sip. After this comes the hard part: each person expresses one personal concern that he asks the others to share with him—not the "missionaries on foreign fields," but something out of his own life. And then (it gets harder) let each person make one personal confession—a weakness or a sin that he needs forgiveness for from God and his brothers and sisters. Could it work? Do we have enough communion now to risk it?

> f. A congregation can enlarge its fellowship
>   by acquainting itself with other congregations.

Do we limit our spiritual community to "our kind of people"? If so, our communion is not of the Spirit or of faith, but perhaps of blood or color. Maybe we should plan some sort of regular meeting with the congregation nearest ours, not merely a pulpit exchange or listening meeting, but a sharing meeting, in which each group shares what the other group looks like to them. Share their joys; share their fears; share their problems. Merely sharing the room while listening to the same speaker is not sharing in communion. If we are going to discover whether communion can cross the borders of congregations, we will have to gather together and share together.

* * *

We have concentrated in this chapter on looking at, listening to, loving, and caring for each other. If this were the whole story, we would achieve nothing more than self-satisfaction. So we close by mentioning something that features prominently in other chapters: service. The best way to get together is to have something to do together for somebody else. We can look at each other best when we also look together to somebody who needs us all. Communion is best when we wear servant's clothes.

We have looked at the life of the church in communion from three points of view. We have seen something of what it is in its spiritual essence. We have seen its earthly reality, and how it does not match that essence. And we have made some suggestions about how we can move things around here and there to help bring the earthly reality closer to the spiritual essence. What we have said in this chapter is only the beginning. The movement from the reality of what the church is like to the ideal of what the communion should be requires imagination. With the end of this chapter we have not spoken the last word on the subject. That is left to the reader.

CHAPTER FOUR

Gathering Together

We live in a broken world whose wounds are full of salt. The hurts of mankind are evident around the globe: wide gaps between races, painful loneliness, grievous oppressions, deep lostness. All the gods men have made for themselves have failed. The world has somehow gone sour and is getting worse. Time is running out. Who has the answers?

Some feel the pain of all this and wonder why we waste time worrying about what Christian people do when they gather together on a Sunday morning. One thing the world does not need, they argue, is the fiddling that the church does in secluded sanctuaries while the world burns. This concern about liturgical gadgetry, this tomfoolery behind stained glass, this pious irrelevance called worship, is an offense, they say. Time is of the essence. If the church is going to be a healing stream in the human desert, it must stop concentrating on what goes on inside its sanctuaries, and leave them to march out into the world where the real action is. Why bother with worship? If we mean to talk in this book about the church's mission in the world, why should we spend a chapter talking about the church's gathering in the sanctuary?

There are two reasons. First of all, everything that the church is and believes and hopes for comes to focus in its meeting on a Sunday morning. Here the core of all that matters gets said and acted out; here the church is brought back anew to the center of its faith; here the church returns from its many-sided work in the world to its only source. If you want to know what any church thinks of itself, its source, and its mission, you can get a good hint from what it does on Sunday when it gathers for worship. That is the first reason for this chapter—to ask whether what we do on Sunday morning *does* in fact express the church's real reason for existence.

Second, we devote a chapter to worship precisely because of the importance of the church's mission in the world. If a battle is going badly, the fault may lie in the generals' command tent. Likewise, if the church is not doing its work well in this hurting, bleeding world of ours, perhaps it is because things are not going well in the control center. When we want to improve parts of the mission of the church, the thing to inquire about first may be the action in the sanctuary. It is there, after all, that the message of our Lord and Commander is laid out.

In order to get a clearer idea of the place of worship in the life of the church, we shall spend the rest of this chapter looking at four major questions about it: What is worship? What goes on when Christians gather together? What standards do we use to evaluate changes in worship practices? How does worship fit into the church's mission to the world?

A. THE SPIRITUAL COMMUNITY WORSHIPS WHEN IT GATHERS TOGETHER.

"Why do we go to church every Sunday, Daddy?" The reply is almost automatic: "Why, we go to church to worship God." The minister begins the service by saying, "Come, let us worship." This is what we do when we gather together: we worship.

Is it really all that simple? If what we do together on Sunday is worship, what is it that we do the rest of the week? Don't we call our gathering the Sunday *service?* Is there really a difference between worship and service? Do we package worship into the holy hour and leave it there? Let us ask another question. Is worship *all* that we do in church? Or, do we worship and do something else?

Your answers to these questions depend on what you think worship is. We do not want to spend time quibbling about words here, but this word is special and merits a longer look.

1. WORSHIP IS ADORING GOD.

Worship is adoration of the holy Lord. The saints in heaven give us the cue. The Lord is in His holy temple, and the Lamb of God is on the throne of glory. What do the people do? They fall on their knees and cry aloud: "Worthy is the Lamb, the Lamb that was slain, to receive all power and wealth, wisdom and might, honor and glory and praise . . . . And the four living creatures said, 'Amen,' and the elders fell down and worshipped."[1]

The Lamb is the worthy one, and worship means to confess His worthiness. Our worship is to glorify His worth-ship. So it was in the temple of Israel. During the sacrifice, the hearts of the people rose up in praise to God like the smoke from the burning coals. The Psalms of Israel everywhere invite us to participate in this adoration: "Ascribe to the Lord the glory due to his name."[2]

Worship is adoring God for the worthy God He is—for His beauty, His goodness, His grace, His holiness. The right posture for it is the bent knee, or the face to the ground. The right mood is awe, wonder, reverence. "The Lord is in his holy temple: let all the earth be hushed in his pres-

[1]Revelation 5:12, 14   [2]Psalm 96:8

ence."[3] If the true end of man is to glorify God, man achieves his final purpose for living—if only for a little while—when he falls on his knees and praises God in the sanctuary.

When people come before the face of God and adore Him in the sanctuary with words of praise ("Holy, Holy, Holy") or awesome silence, they are worshipping God. But this is not all we do at our Sunday service. And this is not all that worship is.

2. WORSHIP IS OBEYING GOD.

Singing psalms of praise within stained glass sanctuaries can be the greatest act man ever does. It can also be hellish nonsense. Certainly God is deserving of every "Worthy art Thou" that arises from our deepest being. But that same cry can come to God like a horrible din. "I hate, I spurn your pilgrim-feasts," He once told Israel. "I will not delight in your sacred ceremonies."[4] "I cannot tolerate your new moons and your festivals; they have become a burden to me and I can put up with them no longer."[5]

If God hated their worship, what did please Him? He says it plainly: "Loyalty is my desire, not sacrifice."[6] "Obedience is better than sacrifice."[7] The missing link between "Come, let us worship" and "I hate your worship" is obedience. The adoration of God in the sanctuary was meant to be the climax of obedience to God in the world. Without the obedience, the hosannas were out of tune. God is not saying that it should be obedience instead of worship, but that obedience is the basis and root of worship.

The New Testament goes further. It tells us that obedience is worship. All of life is swept up toward the throne

[3]Habakkuk 2:20   [4]Amos 5:21   [5]Isaiah 1:14   [6]Hosea 6:6
[7]I Samuel 15:22

and offered as man's real praise to God. Paul puts it this way: "I implore you by God's mercy to offer your very selves to him: a living sacrifice, dedicated and fit for his acceptance, the worship offered by mind and heart."[8]

Worship is what we do with our very selves—always and in all ways. This is the new way that Jesus brought in, making true what the father of John the Baptist prophesied: that the Christ will "grant us, free from fear, to worship him with a holy worship, with uprightness of heart, in his presence, our whole life long."[9] All our lives, all our work, all our play—worship before the face of God. John Calvin knew this well. "The only lawful worship of Him," he said, "is the observation of righteousness, holiness, and piety."

Worship is the obedient, dedicated life. We use the word liturgy to talk about acts of worship. Paul uses a Greek word with the same root when he says that even politicians, ministers of God, are in His service; in other words, His liturgetes.[10] They worshipped, not in the sanctuary, but at city hall. And there was Epaphroditus. He conducted no worship services in our usual sense of the word. But Paul said that Epaphroditus risked his *life* to complete his work of worship for the Philippians.[11] So worship does happen outside the sanctuary out in the world.

Must we then close down the sanctuary? Hardly. Both obedience and worship are what God wants. Adoration without obedience is phony, but work without "the new song" is like music without words.

So worship has two faces: adoration of the Lord in the sanctuary and service of the Lord in the world. But what we do during the Sunday church service is more than worship; that is, not everything in our "worship service" fits under *adoration* of God. Let us look at this a little further.

[8]Romans 12:1   [9]Luke 1:64, 75   [10]Romans 13:6
[11]Read Philippians 2:25-30

B. A VARIETY OF ACTIVITIES TAKE PLACE WHEN THE CHURCH GATHERS TOGETHER.

We should remember two things about the New Testament and worship. First, the people of God worship when they do His will in the world outside the church. Whatever they do inside is not isolated as the only holy thing the church does. Religion or worship is not put in a slot, like the religious section of a Saturday newspaper. All life is sacred, and all life ought to be worship.

Second, the people of God did gather together. The New Testament talks about their "assemblies" and urges Christians not to neglect their gatherings.[1] Paul takes careful note of what the Corinthians do in their gatherings, for he is eager that things be done right.[2] Though worship includes all life lived for God, the Christians did have a special time when they left their separate posts in life to gather together.

Interestingly, the New Testament nowhere uses the name "worship services" for the gatherings. This does not mean that the people did not worship then, but it does hint that they did other things as well.

1. CHRISTIANS ARE TAUGHT ABOUT WHAT GOD DID IN CHRIST.

The message was the core of the gathering. The people came to be briefed again and again, by eyewitness disciples or by gifted teachers. They were told about what God had done in Christ and what He wanted done by Christians. We discussed this activity in Chapter Two, especially in the section on teaching. Recall the description of what the earliest Christians spent their time doing: "They met constantly to hear the apostles teach, and to share the common life . . . ."[3] "Every day they went

[1]Read Hebrews 10:24, 25   [2]See I Corinthians 12-14   [3]Acts 2:42

steadily on with their teaching in the temple and in private houses, telling the good news of Jesus the Messiah."[4]

Teaching was not limited to the assemblies, but one does get the impression that it was especially there that new Christians were taught about the facts of the gospel and their meaning, the will of God for life as a whole. Teaching the truth of God was clearly what happened when Christians came together.

Teaching, we should note, is not worship. Getting briefed is not the same as adoring God in solemn awe. It may be the prelude to worship in the world—getting the will of God clearly, so that we can worship Him at the workbench or in the marketplace. It may also be a prelude to worship in the sanctuary: reminded of who God is and of what He has done, we may be moved to fall on our knees to worship Him. But being taught is different from worshipping.

Are we being taught well? Passing over the question of whether too large a portion of our gatherings is given to teaching and preaching, let us ask whether the teaching is effective.

Today, God's grace has made available to us a number of first-rate teaching aids. Why shouldn't these be used in teaching the greatest message ever heard? Can audio-visual equipment be adapted for use in the sanctuary? Would Paul, who was willing to *be* all things to all men in order to win some, not have *used* all things in order to teach? Furthermore, if teaching is one of the things we do in our gatherings, and if our gatherings are family affairs, shouldn't the children be taught? Don't we teach for the most part as though children were not even present? Good teaching has two parts: it must be true and it must be understood. The church tends to worry a great deal about the first part and pay little mind to the second. But if

[4] Acts 5:42

teaching is crucial, effective teaching is the need of the hour, including the hour of worship.

2. CHRISTIANS CELEBRATE GOD'S SAVING ACTS.

Paul records a direct command from the Lord about what the church should do when it gathers together. "Do this as a memorial of me,"[5] Jesus told the disciples. The church today obeys those words in its celebration of the Lord's Supper. We celebrate because the Lord has *told us* to celebrate.

To celebrate is to recall, in mind and in soul, something wonderful that has happened. What do Christians celebrate? Christian celebration points to something great that happened. It is a celebration of the saving acts of God. It is a *memorial* to Jesus. *Remember:* God was in Christ reconciling the world by the blood of the cross, leading captivity captive, setting loose a new power of salvation in the world, laying the foundations for a new creation. So *celebrate!* Celebrate God's great victory, won through His beloved suffering and dying Son.

Celebration's inner reality is this: when people truly join it, they become part of what is being celebrated. You cannot celebrate truly unless you are in on what the celebration is about. An example from a familiar American event may help illustrate—the old-fashioned Fourth of July celebrations, complete with bands, parades, fireworks, and rousing speeches. When Americans celebrated their national birthday, they did not merely call to mind the sacrifices at Valley Forge. No, there was also pride and thanks at being part of a great land of freedom. To celebrate the Fourth of July was to be and feel like *participants* in all that the birthday of the nation brought forth in this world.

[5] I Corinthians 11:24

It was like this with Israel's Passover celebrations too. When the Jews came together for the Passover, they remembered the great act of God in liberating Israel from Egypt and founding it as His own nation. But they did not just remember what God had done; they also celebrated their participation in God's work. Centuries after the Exodus, the fathers still said to their sons at the Passover, "It is because of what the Lord did for *me* when *I* came out of Egypt." The Passover celebration made people of each new generation part of the saving action.

Paul talks about the Christian celebration this way: "When we bless 'the cup of blessing,' is it not a means of sharing in the body of Christ?"[6] Anyone who celebrates the memorial of Christ is a participant in the great act of God for our salvation. No one really celebrates who is not part of the new work that God began at Calvary. And it works the other way: the celebration makes our participation real to us. It sweeps us up in gratitude and joy at being part of what God has done.

Let us truly celebrate then! The memorial of Christ is not meant to be a mournful hour. We are not to remember Him with tears, not even tears for His terrible suffering. The memorial is a celebration of His victory. Christ has overcome. The future is bright with a living hope. "Overwhelming victory is ours through him who loved us."[7]

Let us return for a moment to our earlier example of celebration. The fireworks on the Fourth of July were not enough; speeches were necessary too. So, too, in celebration of Christ, we need the Word. The sacrament has no meaning by itself; it needs the Word to keep its purpose straight. The sacrament is not a magic power. And it is a solemn occasion. But, having said these things, let us now ask: do we really celebrate when we gather together? "This is the day which the Lord has made; let us *exult* and

[6]I Corinthians 10:16   [7]Romans 8:37

rejoice in it."[8] Our worship services often begin with these words. The Lord's Day, the day He made in victory, the day of hope and joy, is a day of celebration, so we come together to celebrate. But do we celebrate Christ in our church? Would a stranger who knew nothing of what the cross means, coming in on us at our memorial, be able to say: "Whatever these Christians are doing, it is clear they are celebrating something!" Or would he suppose that some sad thing is happening? Can we find ways to put gladness into our memorial?

3. CHRISTIANS BUILD ONE ANOTHER UP.

There were some people in the congregation at Corinth who came together on the Lord's Day and then proceeded to ignore one another. They turned the assemblies into private exercises. Some of them spoke in tongues that nobody else understood. Paul's attitude to this was that it did not help the people build together. To the Corinthians he said, "When a man is using the language of ecstasy he is talking with God, not with men, for no man understands him . . . . The language of ecstasy is good for the speaker himself, but it is prophecy that builds up a Christian community."[9] Paul did not condemn private devotion, not even when it was in "the language of ecstasy." But he did say it had no useful place in the gathering, for we come together to build together.

Who does this building? It is no surprise when it is the messenger, the preacher of the Word, the apostle, the elder, the pastor. This makes sense. But notice how democratic the Spirit is. No one has a monopoly on the job of building. "We ought to see how each of us may best arouse others to love and active goodness, not staying away from our meetings, as some do, but rather encouraging one

[8]Psalm 118:24   [9]I Corinthians 14:2, 4

another all the more because you see the Day drawing near."[10] Encourage one another. Build one another up. Paul says the same thing: "Let the message of Christ dwell among you in all its richness. Instruct and admonish each other with the utmost wisdom . . . ."[11] Admonish one another. Build one another up. Again, Paul says, "of the prophets, two or three may speak, while the rest exercise their judgment upon what is said . . . . You can all prophecy one at a time, so that the whole congregation may receive instruction and encouragement."[12]

Building together. Dare we assume that among today's Christians who gather together there are none whose gifts would help the rest of us? Are there not people who, because of their insights, their experiences, their trials and victories, have something to say to build us up together? Why must the Sunday gathering be a time when such people are silent?

We need not apologize for the educated ministry. We can thank God for men called by Him, dedicated to diligent study of the Scriptures, who lead us into the truth. The message, the proclamation, the sermon—this we need when we come together. But let us not ignore the New Testament pattern. Then Christians gathered together, not only to be instructed by the appointed teacher, not only to celebrate together, but to speak to one another in words that build up the whole Body of Christ. Have we lost those gifts? Is Paul's word to the Romans still a word to us: "I have no doubt in my own mind that you yourselves are quite full of goodness and equipped with knowledge of every kind, *well able to give advice to one another"?*[13]

Paul does not tell us how to organize the building service. What he does tell us is that everything done must "aim at one thing: to build up the church."[14]

[10]Hebrews 10:24, 25   [11]Colossians 3:16   [12]I Corinthians 14:29, 31
[13]Romans 15:14   [14]I Corinthians 14:26

4. CHRISTIAN WORSHIP IS DIALOGUE WITH GOD.

The New Testament gives no blueprint for the things that must be done in our gathering together. Instead, we read a wonderful variety, the specifics of it scattered here and there in the New Testament. The people praised God with songs.[15] They read the Scriptures (the Old Testament), as they were read in the synagogues.[16] They said an Amen, together, to God's Word.[17] They baptized new believers into the name of Jesus.[18] They pleaded with God for the world[19] and for the church.[20]

These are not items listed in a manual of instruction for the gathering, but gleanings from the experience of the church. All of them seemed like natural and necessary things to do when Christians gathered together.

The whole pattern we have been discussing suggests that worship is a dialogue. God is the first speaker. He gives the message. Because He is the holy Lord, in whose house we meet to be reestablished in the power of His Spirit and reconsecrated as members of His new creation, He sets the topics. Because He acted first, He speaks first. He has absolute priority. "We love because he loved us first."[21] But we do not only listen; we are invited to respond. So we talk to Him with praise and petition; we sing to Him and adore Him. Our answers to Him are not limited to the gathering. We answer Him in words at worship and with deeds in the world.

C. CORRECT PATTERNS OF WORSHIP MEET CERTAIN TESTS.

We hear a great deal today about the changes in our world. That all kinds of changes are taking place and will

[15] Ephesians 5:19, 20
[16] I Timothy 4:13; but read also I Thessalonians 5:27
[17] I Corinthians 14:16   [18] I Corinthians 12:13   [19] I Timothy 2:1-7
[20] Acts 2:42   [21] I John 4:19

continue to take place is undeniable. The church, faced by this, must ask itself about changes in its life. And one of the areas in which the call for changes sounds loudest and most often is in the worship of the church.

Resisting change just to keep things as they were is no better than changing for the sake of change. To resist change altogether is likely to mean a loss of power, a loss of people—especially young people—and, what is most important, a loss of ability to carry out the mission to the changing world.

But change ought to come in response to needs, real needs of real people to worship in a real way in our time. And the response must come as Christian people respond together to the impulse of the Spirit.

We said that the Bible gives us no blueprint for an unchanging way of doing things in the gathering. But there are guidelines to help us as we change. As we face the invasion of the future into our church life, we do well to keep some test questions in mind.

1. WHAT HAPPENS MUST BUILD.

This is Paul's primary standard for judging what happens in the gathering. After noting the various (and sometimes strange) goings-on in the church at Corinth, he sets forth a principle: "All of these must aim at one thing: to build up the church."[1]

Now if this guideline is going to help us, we have to take a close look at the notion of building. Building up is not the same as prettying up or "redecorating" the liturgy. Such surface changes add nothing to the strength of the structure. Building up does not aim at making people feel good inside. The biblical notion of building up requires that it be *for* something. Christian people are to be built up for service.

[1] I Corinthians 14:26

There is a fight to be fought. There is work to be done, love to share, life to give. There is a witness that must go out, hurts that must be healed, souls that must be saved. So to test what is done in the gathering, we simply ask: does it build up the people of God for doing the work of God in their time and place?

2. WHAT HAPPENS MUST CELEBRATE.

Another test of the rightness of change is this: does it help the congregation sound its Hallelujah to the Lamb of God? Does it contribute to celebration? Does it help us celebrate the only thing that we can celebrate without reservations?

Joyful sounds alone are not enough. The crucial point here is that the message must be at the heart of the celebration. This is what Christians celebrate when they gather together—the gospel of the Lordship of Jesus Christ—and that message may never be toned down or tuned out by the celebration.

But if joyful sounds are not by themselves indicators that the celebration is on the right track, any trend toward gloom, sadness, and grim despair is a sure indicator that the gathering has taken a wrong turn. If what we do in church gives off the atmosphere of weary sobriety or defeated joylessness, we have left the mainline of New Testament gatherings.

The world outside of Christ is a world of despair. Even its make believe is without hope, without prospect. Life outside of Christ is life pregnant with reason for fear, heavy with cause for anxiety. But the Christian congregation looks directly at sin and death, frustration and fear, and then turns and sounds a Hallelujah to Him who overcame. Our theme is the Easter message. Our key is joy. If we do not demonstrate that by what we do in church, we have lost the first round to the world.

3. WHAT HAPPENS MUST KEEP THE ENTIRE CONGREGATION IN MIND.

In order to be pastoral, the change must be made with the whole congregation in mind, the particular congregation that gathers together. The right way to test any change in liturgy is to ask whether it is made out of concern for the good of all.

Some of the people in the congregation are children. Do our gatherings demonstrate that we are really concerned for them? Can they understand the instruction? Can they really join the celebration? Is it attuned to their needs and their capacity? Others are youth. Do our gatherings embrace them? Are they really present in more than their bodies? What about their idiom, their dress, their tempo? Others of the people are old, and old people are as precious as young people. Do our changes respect their temperament and needs, even their need for stability and regular patterns?

Behind all these specific questions lies a more crucial general one: how do we know what people need? Can everything be settled in consistory or church board meetings? Do people have a chance to tell the church? Do all the people—young and old alike—have a voice in the gatherings?

We should bear in mind not only that people within one congregation are different from one another, but also that congregations differ from one another. Some communities are on the move into the future; others have their hearts in the past. What is a good change for one may be disastrous for another. But as Calvin said, if we let love be our guide, we will not go far wrong.

4. WHAT HAPPENS MUST BE CONFESSIONAL.

Christians gather together as a people committed to a confession. Every congregation believes certain truths about God and man and itself, and it expresses these beliefs in creeds. What we do in our gatherings ought at least to be consistent with and at most to express what we believe and what we are. What we do must demonstrate what we are, what our faith affirms, what our hope is, and where our calling lies. Any changes in our worship must bear that in mind.

5. WHAT HAPPENS MUST BE CATHOLIC.

We come together as Christians. This means that Christians from any place or time ought to be able to recognize our gathering as being Christian—as done "in the name of the Lord Jesus." We do not come together to celebrate our national heritage or our ethnic origin or even our sectarian specialties. We come as believers in the Lord Jesus Christ, members of His universal family. That family goes back into the past as well as around the world. Our gatherings must be part of a line that leads through all the gatherings of the past. Tradition has its place; and if we give tradition its place, it will keep us from novelty for the sake of novelty. Is it catholic? This is one test of good change.

6. WHAT HAPPENS MUST BE BIBLICAL.

The Bible is our center; by it everything else is controlled. From the Bible we know why we worship, whom we worship, and what the themes of our gatherings are. All the other standards we have mentioned are really subpoints under this one.

If our worship is biblical, it will be simple and clear. If it is biblical, it will always point to Jesus Christ. If it is biblical, it will always be appropriate to loving concern for the people.

D. THE CHURCH GATHERS AWAY FROM THE WORLD IN ORDER TO GO BACK INTO IT.

We gather together, not simply to have a good time in celebration. We gather away from the world in order to get back in again. We draw apart in order better to engage in service for the world. When we leave the assembly, we are dismissed to mission.

1. THE GATHERING IS A FAMILY AFFAIR.

When the church assembles, it does so as the family of God. Like human families, we do things together; and one has to be in the family to be part of the celebration. The family gathers to get the Word from its Father in heaven.

The church does not gather for evangelism. The Sunday meeting is not a missionary event, but the gathering of those who already belong to the new creation in Christ. It is a family affair.

But what family turns away a guest? And where can a stranger better discover the power behind the family than at the family gathering? This is why what we do must reveal what we are in Christ; why the message must be clear and simple; why, in a world enslaved to defeat, our gatherings must explode with joy and hope; in short, why everything we do must point straight to the center: Jesus Christ, the crucified and risen Lord.

2. CHRISTIANS WHO GATHER TOGETHER TURN TO GOD IN CONCERN FOR THE WORLD.

In the gathering, Christians get their briefing and their Spirit-stimulation for mission in the world. But even in the gathering, they are turned toward God in deep concern for the world.

46036

The gathering is no more a retreat from the world than the Lord's return to heaven was a forsaking of the world. At church, the people join Him in His priestly prayer for the needs of all men. Christian people do in the sanctuary what Jeremiah told the Hebrew exiles to do in the situations in which they found themselves: "Seek the welfare of any city to which I have carried you off, and pray to the Lord for it; on its welfare your welfare will depend."[1] In their gatherings, Christians follow Paul's instructions: "I urge that petitions, prayers, intercession, and thanksgiving be offered for all men .... Such prayer is right, and approved by God our Saviour, whose will it is that all men should find salvation and come to know the truth."[2]

What happens within the assembly—the effective prayers of God's people—is pivotal for missions. Calvin puts the combination—assembly and mission—in perspective: "Quickened and stirred by the reading and preaching of the Gospel and the confession of our faith ... it follows that we must pray for the salvation of all men .... Now, the life of Christ consists in this, namely to seek and to save that which is lost; fittingly, then, we pray for all men."

We do more than pray. We give for the needs of the world. A test of whether we do the right thing in the assembly is the test of giving. Where does the money go? Is it made clear that we are giving for those who are hurting and dying and lost? Too often in our churches, offerings are designated for "general expenses." How can we really celebrate in our giving if we give for "general expenses," which include only anonymously the cause of missions? If our giving is to be celebration, we ought to give out of the fulness of Christ for needs that we *know* about. How can we give in compassion, if all we know is that we are giving for "general expenses"? Perhaps the deacons ought to

[1] Jeremiah 29:7   [2] I Timothy 2:1, 3

participate in our gatherings by telling the people about the specific *needs* of real people for the gifts of the church.

*   *   *

What we do in the assembly tells us—and the world—what we are. And it tells us what to do when we are dispersed. The world will soon know whether our gathering together means service for the world or just service for ourselves.

Do we assemble to celebrate? Do we assemble for briefing from the Word for the world? Do our gatherings build us up for Christian service? These are questions that each congregation must answer for itself.

CHAPTER FIVE

Structures of Life

We all have a good idea of what structures are. Buildings, for example, are structures. They have walls that close people in. So, on the one hand, a building limits freedom. But on the other hand, a building gives one freedom to do things inside its walls that he cannot do outside, freedom to do one's work, enjoy one's family, and live as one wants to live. Structures do both: they fence us in and they set us free.

Our concern in this chapter, of course, is not primarily with buildings. We are talking about ourselves as the people of God and about the structures we build for our life and work together. We use some of the same kind of language as we do when we talk about buildings, but we mean the solid, steady, regular ways in which the church carries on its service. Structures are the ways people organize to keep getting their work done.

To get a better idea of what some church structures are, ask yourself a few questions. Do you have to guess on Sunday morning when the service will begin that day? Do you have any doubt about what, in general, will happen at church, or is the pattern quite set from Sunday to Sunday? Are you left in the dark about who makes the important decisions for your church, or are you rather sure about the elders? Do you have to guess who takes the collection, counts the money, and sees to its proper use, or do you leave that to the deacons? And beyond your local congregation, you know about classis, and Synod, and numerous denominational boards and committees. All run on time, dependably and regularly. Of the many structures in the church these are a few with which we are all acquainted.

Structures, then, are ways that people who work together organize to get their work done efficiently. Once a pattern is established, once it is in use for a long time, it is called a structure. There is nothing mysterious or sinister about structures as such. They are not bad—or good—in themselves. They are merely ways that we have discovered, or were given, for getting done the work God gave us to do.

Yet people are very sensitive about structures these days. Students feel frustrated by the rigid structures of the university or multiversity. Some have fled the structures of society to live in communes, without any structures. Others want to destroy existing structures. The peaceful commune-dweller, the bomb-throwing revolutionary, the protesting student—all oppose structures because they believe that structures destroy freedom and inflict oppression.

This feeling has arisen in the churches too. There are many who feel that rigid patterns of church life have taken away the freedom of the Spirit. Others feel that some structures are all right, but that the ones we have are obsolete, no longer useful in our time. Are these critics correct? Are the structures of the church today prisons of the Spirit? Are they ways that were once useful but are now out of date? Do they stifle the Spirit? Do they shackle the church? Let us look at these questions.

A. THE SPIRIT CREATES STRUCTURES
   FOR THE CHURCH.

The Spirit means freedom. "Where the Spirit of the Lord is, there is liberty."[1] Surely the Spirit does not build

[1] II Corinthians 3:17

fences to close us in. No, He breaks down walls to set us free. For He is free, wonderfully free, like the wind, which blows "where it wills; you hear the sound of it, but you do not know where it comes from, or where it is going."[2] Paul tells us to be free, not to be tied down by human structures.[3]

How different things seem to be in our churches. One can predict almost everything, even the length of the sermon. Try to get things changed—even a little thing like the date of a meeting or the order of worship—and you will find out how tight and firm the walls of the structure are. Can this be the church indwelt by the free Spirit?

But perhaps we have an incorrect notion of the Spirit and His freedom. Is freedom really the enemy of order, and is order really against freedom? Remember how the Spirit in the beginning brooded over the waters of chaos— they were free, in a sense—and brought order out of the waste. With His creative act He brought structure into life. The Creator Spirit moves the sun, and the earth around it, in so orderly a way that we measure time by its movement. Without structure in nature we would die. The Spirit of Lord, the free Spirit, is also the Creator Spirit. He is not against order; He creates it.

When the risen Jesus sent His free Spirit to the church, He did not tear down order. We cannot possibly read the Book of Acts and come away thinking that the Spirit hates organization. The church did not grow and meet new challenges along the way just by chance. "Let all be done decently and in order," said Paul.[4] This, he was certain, was the way to respond to the Spirit.

The first synod of the church is reported in Acts 15. Was this the bright idea of some organization man? The church did not think so; they looked on it as the Spirit's work. It was the beginning of structure, but it was not an establish-

2John 3:8   3Read Galatians 4:28-5:1   4I Corinthians 14:40

ment takeover that stifled the Spirit. "It is the decision of the Spirit, and our decision," the apostles and elders concluded.[5] Synods and the Spirit can work together, not for killing freedom, but for freely advancing the Kingdom.

When the poor were not being cared for effectively, the Spirit's response was to appoint men to take care of the job in particular; that is, He established a structure.[6] It was the Spirit who personally designated Paul and Barnabas to the regular task of missions.[7] When the church needed pastoral care, elders were appointed—and care was taken to do things in good order.[8] There are recognized leaders and recognized followers; and Paul did not hesitate to exert his authority within the structure.

We conclude that the Spirit, the author of freedom, does not tear down structures, but creates them. Structures, as such, are not the enemy of freedom, for freedom is not chaos or disorder. Freedom needs order and structures. Our freedom is for service, and when the people of God, together, are called to serve God in our world, we need structures.

B. THE STRUCTURES OF THE CHURCH MUST ARISE FROM ITS NEEDS.

How and why does the Spirit create structures? Does He want us to build unchangeable structures? We shall consider in this section how the structures of the church must be related to needs.

1. OFFICES IN THE CHURCH ARE DESIGNATED FOR GETTING ACCOMPLISHED WHAT MUST BE DONE.

When the Spirit created structures, He was responding to needs. He gave gifts as they were needed, and the kind

[5] Acts 15:28   [6] Read Acts 6:5, 6   [7] Acts 13:1-3
[8] Read I Timothy 3:1-7; Titus 1:5-9

of gifts He gave were determined by the needs of the church.

The Spirit gave people to do certain types of work for the church. Since they filled these jobs regularly, we call some of these jobs offices. Note this well: offices are only designated and recognized jobs or duties. We can say, then, that the Spirit gave offices, and that these offices form parts of the structure. But we must remember that filling a need was always the reason behind this.

The Spirit did not give gifts merely to get things organized. The organization was only the means; meeting the need of the church was the end. "These were his gifts: some to be apostles, some prophets, some evangelists, some pastors and teachers, *to equip God's people for work in his service, to the building up of the body of Christ.*"[1] The need was present; then God's Spirit provided men to fill the need. The need determined the kind of gift, and the gift created the structure.

We see the same pattern almost everywhere. When things were going badly in the care for the poor because the apostles were not using their time well in caring for widows, the Spirit added to the structure by appointing seven men to this particular task, forerunners of our deacons. The elders, too, were appointed for a purpose. False teaching spread like an epidemic if devoted minds were not posted to ward it off. Elders were chosen with great care, and guarding against heresy was one of their main tasks.[2] These special jobs were set within a structure because this was clearly the most effective way of getting the task done.

We do not ordinarily think of a body as a structure, but the two do have some things in common. In both there are order, specialization, and differentiation—all for the service of the whole. So, Paul distinguishes the various gifts in the

[1]Ephesians 4:12   [2]Read Titus 1:9

Body of Christ. People have different gifts, as individuals. And each of them is called to use his gifts. Each at his place, each with his gifts, functions with all the others to keep the Body at work, growing, and ministering to the world for Jesus Christ.[3]

2. THE ORGANIZATION OF THE CHURCH IS FLEXIBLE.

One thing is stressed here: structure is given to the church to serve a purpose. For this reason, the organization of the church in the New Testament is fluid. The disciples did not begin by appointing a committee to write a constitution that would fix and settle the organization from the beginning and for all time. The church started out with little thought for structure. Who would think of organization in the full, life-giving torrent of the Spirit? But as the church grew, and as it went out into the world, new needs arose. And the needs invited the addition of offices, which the Spirit provided by giving gifts to men to fit them for the offices (duties).

We notice a kind of vagueness about the way in which each gift was to be used. There was a job that needed to be done, but we do not get the impression that the job description was detailed or set out for all time. A measure of adaptability was expected. Take the elders, for example. Nothing is said about how many were needed or how often they were to meet together (if ever) or what their precise relationship was to other offices. No rules were given for them to care for the sacraments or make family visits or hire preachers. Much seems to be left to the loving will, the will to serve the church in its changing needs. The same thing can be said for all the offices.

It is not as clear as we sometimes think which offices were meant to be permanent and which were only for the time being. The church is probably correct in holding that

[3] Read I Corinthians 12:4-10

the tasks of elders, deacons, and pastors are permanent. But are we absolutely sure that there is no place for healing, for prophecy, or for discerners of spirits?

3. NEEDS CHANGE; THEREFORE, STRUCTURES CHANGE TO MEET THEM.

If the structure is given in order to meet the needs of the church—if this is the New Testament pattern—does it not make sense for us to let needs shape the structure today? Needs change. True, the need for keeping the message clear and pure does not change; the need to care for the poor does not change. But the *form* of many needs changes, because the social setting of the church has changed. Consider some examples. Today's church needs a committee for maintaining the building and grounds, but the New Testament church, meeting in the houses of Christian people, did not. We need committees to arrange car pools, address letters, provide the elements for the sacrament, clean up the kitchen, and care for Sunday Schools and choirs. All of these are sparked by changing needs. Perhaps we ought to consider the whole structure of the church in terms of whether it answers the changing needs of the people—the people of the church and the people we are summoned to reach in the world. If we think more of needs than of keeping the organization running smoothly, we will be ready to respond more swiftly to the Spirit's gifts.

C. MISSION IS THE PRIMARY CONCERN OF THE CHURCH'S STRUCTURES.

1. THE SPIRITUAL COMMUNITY IS ELECTED BY GOD FOR MISSION.

We all know that the church has a mission in the world. We said in the first chapter that the church does not decide whether or not to have a mission, that it was chosen by God to perform His mission. The church does not decide for itself what sort of mission it must perform; its mission was given by God. Perhaps the most crucial need of the church is for gifts to perform that mission in the world.

The church is the gathering of God's elect people, called out of the world by the gospel to be God's own family to His everlasting praise. The church is God's *elect community*. To some, this is the end of the matter. Once the church was formed, its task was to preserve the elect from sin and stain. Its structure was fashioned for security purposes: to mind the walls of Zion, to defend against invasion by the armies of Satan. Now it is certainly true that the need for securing the walls is real. But is this a complete picture?

To be chosen is a privilege. The people of the elect community know they are forgiven and made new only because God freely and sovereignly chose them in love. But the biblical truth is that to be elect is to be called to a mission. We have all our blessings in Christ because God chose us in Christ.[1] His choice is a commission to service. "You did not choose me; I chose you. I appointed you *to go on and bear fruit, fruit that shall last.*"[2] Election is two-directional; it involves both God's choice of us and His mission for us.

Israel got the lines of their election badly tangled. We can learn from their mistake. They were always going overboard on the privilege side of election. They were the chosen people, and they were proud of it. They were secure in the confidence that nothing could change God's mind once it was made up. Nothing could count against them anymore. Nothing could blot out this simple fact: God had elected them and, despite sin and injustice, noth-

---

[1] Read Ephesians 1:4   [2] John 15:16

ing would change. Imagine, then, how they felt when they heard one of their prophets give this interpretation of what election meant: "For you alone have I cared among all the nations of the world; *therefore will I punish you.*"[3] Election entailed responsibility; failure to respond to the call meant that punishment was on its way.

Israel was called to be God's servant to the world, the witness to the freedom of God's grace and the goodness of God's will. Imagine a man selected to be a cabinet member by a newly elected President or Premier. What a privilege! But suppose he accepted the honor and never showed up for duty. He would have missed the whole point. He was chosen—and this was a privilege—but the whole point of being chosen was to perform a service for his country. This, in effect, was what Israel did. They loved the privilege, but forgot that the privilege was the privilege of serving the Lord God among the Gentiles.

That is the idea of election that prevails in the New Testament. "You are a chosen race . . . , a people claimed by God for his own," Peter tells the Christians, "*to proclaim. . . .*"[4] You can take all the demands that the Lord lays on the church, sum them up, and say: this is the purpose of our election. "Bear fruit"[5] or "make all nations my disciples"[6] or "proclaim the triumphs of him who has called you out of darkness"[7] or "be dedicated . . . , without blemish in his sight . . . , full of love"[8]—all of these tell us why we were elected by God in His free, eternal love.

One does not cancel the other out. We look only to God's loving choice to explain our surprising status as God's children. But God's summons to serve is the explanation of God's election. To put it another way: we do not know why God chose *us*, but we do know why God *chose* us.

3Amos 3:2   4I Peter 2:9   5John 15:16   6Matthew 28:19
7I Peter 2:9   8Ephesians 1:4

The elect people have a mission in the world. And the questions about the church's structure have to be answered by our needs to perform our mission. We are elect to serve; and the world we serve is a changing world. How do our inherited structures help or hinder our service to our world in our time?

2. THE CHURCH IS CREATED
BY THE LIFE-GIVING SPIRIT FOR MISSION.

The church was chosen by the Father from eternity, redeemed by the Son at Calvary, and created by the Spirit at Pentecost. The Spirit brings the risen, victorious life of Jesus Christ into the broken humanity of sinful believers and joins them together in the new creation, the Body of Christ. We may never separate the Spirit from Christ in our thought, because the Spirit is never separate from Christ in reality. This is why the church is Christ's Body.

The one thing that is new about the church is the reality of the Spirit's life. He is the "life-giving Spirit."[9] But life is never meant to be wrapped in blankets, to be kept aloof, alone, unshared. The Spirit creates new life in the church so that life can be shared. You cannot have the Spirit without sharing His life. If you are in the stream of the Spirit, it will carry you to others. So it lies in the very essence of the church to be in mission. It is not a thing the church can decide to do or not do. If the church is the creation of the Spirit, it will be the church in mission.

Structures are part of this picture. To try to get the church into mission by tinkering with the structure of the church is to put the cart before the horse. No church has ever become a missionary church because someone adjusted the machinery. Changes in structure come about when the Spirit moves the church into new situations to meet new needs. They are responses to power; they can

[9] I Corinthians 15:45

never generate power. But when the power is present and the needs change, the church will be able to accept new structures.

Structures can also get in the way of the church in mission to the world. A church may be structured so formally that the spontaneous fellowship of God's people is prevented. Or its structures may be so limited to tasks within the church that the mission to the needs of men outside the church is not fulfilled. Structures like this become obstacles that prevent God's mission from happening and quench the Holy Spirit.

3. MEN ARE RENEWED BY THE SPIRIT THROUGH THE WORK OF THE CHURCH.

God's purpose is plain: to create a new humanity in Christ. The church is called to be the front-runner in His program. Anyone who wants to know what God has done, is doing, and is going to do in Christ should be able to get the answer by looking at the church. The task of the church is to respond to the Word and Spirit in such a way that it will be the new humanity in visible form. Read the words of Paul carefully, and let them sink into your mind: "Gentiles and Jews, he has made the two one, and in his own body of flesh and blood has broken down the enmity which stood like a dividing wall between them; for he annulled the law with its rules and regulations, *so as to create out of the two a single new humanity* . . . . This was his purpose . . . ."[10]

A single new humanity. Any person in Christ is a new creature, and the new creatures joined in Christ's Body are the new humanity.

Note well: this new humanity is a newly human fellowship of restored persons, not of angels, not of perfectly

10Ephesians 2:14-16

new people—yet. In the new humanity the wounds that sin inflicted begin to be healed; the walls that sin built between men begin to crumble; the love that sin distorted begins to straighten out. Here the honesty that sin prevented begins to assert itself. Here men begin to accept each other, help each other, forgive each other, love each other—in Christ. The church is the Body of Christ, where people belong to one another because they share His Spirit.

This is the point for missions. The church that shows signs that the Kingdom of God has come is already engaged in mission just by *being* the new humanity. It is a visible sign of the invisible power of God. Where the new creation is really alive and visible in the congregation of Christ, mission is being carried on. This cannot be all. Words have to be spoken; a witness of the written Word and the acted Word must follow. But *being* God's new humanity in a fractured, hostile, lonely, cruel society is the first and basic step in mission.

What does this have to do with structure? Tampering with the gadgetry of organization cannot create the new humanity. Newness in men is the work of the Spirit—along with the reality of man's faith and obedience. But the structure must be ready to bend to the currents of life that stir among the people, ready to change as the Spirit urges them on to new and more genuine outbursts of the newness of life in Christ. We must set the priorities straight: structure *follows* need. To meet man's need, God made Himself known in human form, the form of the New Man, Jesus Christ. God's people today must meet human need by demonstrating—now, in our time—the redeemed human society.

This is quite different from a demonstration of efficient organization. It does not have to do with large building programs or high budgets or any of the statistics that newspapers like to report. The world may be impressed—

and it usually is—with success stories. But the sign of the Spirit, the demonstration of the new creation, is seen in the love we have for one another, the unstinted generosity, the open embrace of *all* men, the bearing of burdens for others, the willingness to suffer for Jesus Christ. This is what the church needs to make the new humanity visible to the world.

And the church must be willing to accept any gifts that the Spirit brings, any changes in structure, any realignment of its organization, that will help meet this need.

D. THE CHURCH MUST CHANGE IN ORDER TO MEET THE NEEDS OF THE FUTURE.

1. THROUGH RAPID CHANGES, THE FUTURE HAS INVADED THE PRESENT.

The future has caught up with us all. Change—radical and shocking—is the definition of life. Most of what has happened in the history of the world has happened in the lifetime of the average church member. The future is not something far ahead of us; it has invaded our present time. It has come so fast that children cannot even comprehend, let alone admire, the childhood world of their parents.

The change of life extends from top to bottom. It ranges from the moon to morals, from technology to toilet training, from computer programming to family planning. Nobody knows what the future will bring us tomorrow; we do know that the future has invaded us today. We are experiencing a revolution so fundamental that we can hardly find a parallel in all of human history. The world of our children is as different from the world of our childhood as the world of Julius Caesar was different from the world we were born into.

We need not document the extent and depth of change here. But reflect on just a few items. The country is becoming citified. Not only are people moving to the city; the city is moving to the country. Ninety-two percent of all our population growth since 1910 has been in large cities. But that is only part of it. Through television, transistor radios, and movies, the city has taken over the heart and mind of the country. There is a steadily diminishing difference between the city dweller and the country dweller. All have taken over the mind and heart of the city.

Or consider technology. Nobody can really grasp or even imagine what technology is doing to us; slave or liberator or both, it is turning life inside out. The simplest form of change here is speed of travel. In 6,000 B.C. the fastest form of travel was by camel—at eight miles per hour. It took more than four thousand years to increase that speed to twenty miles per hour by chariot. By 1825, nearly four thousand years later, the first steam engine made all of thirteen miles per hour. But a little more than one hundred years after that, men could fly at four hundred miles per hour. Less than thirty years later—in the 1960s—we multiplied that speed by ten, and flew four thousand miles per hour. And, with an enormous blast of energy, some men have circled the earth at 18,000 miles per hour.

But speed of travel is the simplest form of change. There is the information explosion. Nobody can keep up with the growth of information anymore. The informed man of yesterday is the obsolete man of today. There is the mobility of society. More families are on the move today than in all history. Community is destroyed by constant movement. There is trouble in the family. Families have been fractured by technology. The mystery of birth and death is gone from the family—all of it happens away from home, in some clinical setting to which children are not admitted. Roots are pulled up, and the small, nuclear family is left on its own to find resources within itself for survival. More and more families are not surviving.

Or consider morals. There was a time when the church taught people how to live by teaching them the will of God for life. Even when they stopped listening to the church, people still believed in some sort of moral code, lodged in nature or the conscience. Today, change is the norm and liberty the rule. Where are eternal norms, abiding principles, changeless codes in a world where change is ultimate? The question is no longer what ought to be done because it is the right thing to do. The question is: what can be done to bring the greatest satisfaction right now? Not what rules demand, but what freedom delivers; not what law decrees, but what feelings desire; not what is right, but what is personally satisfying. This is the code of the future.

Can the church structure itself so that it will be the new, Christ-created humanity within the crazy mixed-up world of tomorrow that has come on us today? Can the church structure itself to missions within this world where the future rushes into the present? The answer is Yes, it can. The church *will* restructure its life—whether it decides to or not; the only question is whether it will change in order to serve, or change—later rather than sooner—only because it too reflects the changes of the world within it.

2. WE MUST BE READY TO ACCEPT THE SPIRIT'S GIFTS TO RESTRUCTURE THE CHURCH.

The church must come to terms with change so that it can minister to changing people in a changing world. But it must also change in order to minister effectively to the people within its membership. We can speak of inner-directed and outer-directed change.

It would be futile to try to engineer in advance the changes that must be made if the church is really going to minister to the needs of its future members—our children. We will have to be hard at prayer, waiting for the Spirit to lead and provide. Tinkering is not the answer. But readiness to follow, willingness to listen, and a relaxed grip on our present structures are the beginning of the answer.

Let us consider some examples. Begin with little things which often sound like radical things. There is absolutely nothing sacred or biblical about pipe organs. Why, then, should their solemn strains—or sentimental gushings—dominate the high moments of worship for people whose hearts and feet are tuned to drum and guitar? What about the monopoly on the Word that the preacher has? Can we admit the reality of the prophetic office of all believers? Can we let the Word come back to the pulpit from the pews as well as from pulpit to pew? Will we listen to Paul: "Instruct and admonish each other"?[1] What about clothes? Will we always have to "dress up" in Sunday best for God's house—the house of the God who does not look on the outward appearance, but looks within? Will Sunday service always have to be an hour to an hour-and-a-quarter, twice a Sunday, or are we willing to do it differently?

What about buildings? Must the church go on issuing promissory notes to pay for bigger and bigger buildings for itself? Will future generations be impressed by the people of God struggling not to serve the world, but to pay off the mortgage on their edifice? Do the followers of Him who had no house to call His own—not even a pillow for His head—have to invest precious resources to build more stately mansions at a time when building costs are sky (not heaven) high? Are we willing to meet the future in a rented building? Or can we build a complex—a kind of churchly condominium—for several congregations to share? Can we restructure the physical structure?

The question is not what we can do to make it work,

[1]Colossians 3:16

but what we are willing to do when the Spirit calls us to work.

Now, let us think outward. The difference between inner-directed and outer-directed change is mostly a matter of emphasis. What we are willing to change for the sake of ministry to the world is not absolutely different from what we must be willing to do for building up the Body within.

The world "out there" is a world of families coming apart. Even if divorce has not broken the home, the members of many families live in different worlds from one another. How can the church adapt itself to minister to the fractured family? One way would be to go along with the trend and forget the family, concentrating our efforts on individuals. But the family—however it takes shape—is clearly the base of God's operation in the world. The church must minister to the family, not undermine it. The question is how the church can structure its program to fulfil its mission to the family.

It will not be enough to get families to church for worship on Sunday if what happens there does not speak to the whole family, including the children. Even so, it is unlikely that we can bring the entire family in. What about organizing the weekday life of the church to provide for a family service? Professional counseling has its place, but Christian sharing has its place too—maybe a better one. Parents could meet according to the ages of their children; for instance, parents of teen-agers could meet together to share their problems and tears. An unchurched set of parents may well be more impressed by Christian parents admitting their dilemmas and looking to God and to each other for support than by a hundred sermons on the duties and glories of parenthood. The price is honesty, humility, and enormous love and trust of one another. It may be that parents talking together—with the assist of a prophetic Word—about their common anguish or common joy may be one of the strategic structures of tomorrow's church.

This may be the church's leverage for mission to the family fractured by today's secularized urban culture.

What about vocation? There was a time when the men of the church met together on Tuesday night to debate the deep issues of doctrine. If a citizen of today's secular world dropped in on such a society meeting, he would think he had landed in a secret meeting of foreigners from a strange land. Tomorrow's church may not have the luxury of merely getting together for Bible lessons and doctrinal forays. We may have to structure our clubs and societies for mission to the world.

But mission is a big, all-embracing task with many branches. Our groupings may have to be made on vocational lines—not according to what a man does for a living, but according to what he can do for his mission in the world for Christ. The Spirit gives many kinds of gifts and inspires many kinds of opportunities. Maybe people will have to get together on the basis of what they can *do.* Mothers could be organized for ministry to the sick or to children spiritually deserted or to divorced mothers; or for helping one another learn to witness with words as real people. Men could be organized according to *their* mission vocation: learning to work in the ghetto, ministering within politics, or communicating the gospel to labor unions. All of these are tough assignments, but the church has to be willing to shift priorities to meet them.

This may demand more flexibility than we have ever dreamed of. People may have to move about, depending on where they are needed. Not every congregation is large enough to perform a total mission by itself, so members may have to cross congregational lines, getting together for mission, not according to where their membership happens to be registered, but according to how they can serve.

Enough has been said to raise this question: are we ready to accept the Spirit's gifts to restructure the church to meet the needs of people in tomorrow's world? The fact is that tomorrow's world is here now, and the structures *are* beginning to change already. The phenomenal rise in "growth groups" in many congregations shows that the structure *is* changing. Many churches are seeking, praying, struggling to find right adjustments, fruitful shifts, in structure. "Where the Spirit of the Lord is, there is liberty."[2] And that includes liberty to change the structures.

* * *

Change for the sake of change is stupid and fruitless. Just as tinkering with the radiator cap on a car will not fill an empty gas tank, so tinkering with the structures of the church will not fill us with the Spirit. Where the Spirit is not powerfully present, there is neither freedom nor fruitfulness. Moreover, some things must not and cannot change. The message is the same because what God did and is doing is the same; only the vocabulary, the style, and the context change. The secret power of love does not change; only the ways that love is shared change.

Recall what the church is—the Body of our Lord Jesus Christ. One thing about bodies is universally true: they have to adapt. If they do not adapt to changing conditions, they are immobilized at best and they die at worst. If the church is the Body of Christ, it is adaptable. And if it is to fill Christ's mission to the world it must adapt, not to the world's spirit, but for mission to the world's needs.

[2] II Corinthians 3:17

The Way

CHAPTER SIX

The Way of a Servant

Imagine that all the population of the world were condensed to the size of one village of one hundred people. In this village, 67 of the 100 people would be poor; the other 33 would be, in varying degrees, well-off. Of the total population, only seven would be North Americans. The other 93 people would watch the seven North Americans spend one-half of all the money, eat one-seventh of all the food, and use one-half of all the bathtubs. These seven people would have ten times more doctors than the other 93. Meanwhile, the seven would continue to get more and more, and the 93 less and less.

This unequal distribution of wealth has an effect on us as church members. As part of the wealthy seven, we are trying to reach as many of the other 93 for Christ as we can. We tell them about Jesus, and they watch us throw away more food than they ever hope to eat. We are busy building beautiful church buildings, and they scrounge to find shelter for their families. We have money in the bank, and they do not have enough to buy food for their children. All the while, we tell them that our Master was the Servant of men, the Savior who gave His all for us and bids us give all for Him.

How do we, in that situation, arrange the life of our church, the life we live, in order to win the 93 for Christ and the new life in Him? We are the rich minority in the world. We may be able to forget about that or consider it unimportant. The question is, can the 93 forget?

A. THE WAY OF THE CHURCH IS THE WAY OF A SERVANT.

We proclaim Christ in this world. And our Lord Jesus said that a servant does not rank above his master.[1] How can we be less than the master who is the servant of men? This is the question we ask in this chapter.

1. JESUS CAME CONQUERING WITH THE SIGN OF A TOWEL.

The Jews of Jesus' time kept asking Him for a sign, a signal to prove who He really was. He refused to give them the kind of sign they wanted, but He did give a sign that identifies Him plainly. Everything He was and did, and is and does, is signaled to us by one gesture—the sign of the towel.

The night before His crucifixion Jesus performed one menial task that told the story of His life and summarized all of His mission. "During supper, Jesus . . . rose from table, laid aside his garments, and taking a towel, tied it round him. Then he poured water in a basin, and began to wash his disciples' feet and to wipe them with the towel."[2]

When He had finished this humble chore, He asked whether the disciples understood what He had done. They probably did not. So He told them: "You call me 'Master' and 'Lord,' and rightly so, for that is what I am. Then if I, your Lord and Master, have washed your feet, you also ought to wash one another's feet."[3]

The sign of the towel has to be the badge for every Christian, every church. There is no escape clause, no way

[1] Read Matthew 10:24, 25   [2] John 13:3-5   [3] John 13:13, 14

of dodging this unsettling fact: Jesus wears the badge of the servant, and we must wear it too. If we refuse, we turn Christian reality upside down. If we turn away the towel, we really claim that what Jesus said was not true after all: we claim that the servant really outranks the Master. And that is to deny the Lord.

Jesus' identity is made transparent by the sign of the towel. His words and His deeds said it over and over again: "Here am I among you like a servant."[4] *Like a servant*—not at a church supper once a month, but as a way of life. "The Son of Man . . . did not come to be served, but to serve, and to give up his life as a ransom for many."[5] What He said, He did. There is no hint that Jesus ever tried to advance His status, promote His ambitions, or get ahead for Himself. He lived to serve; He came to be a slave. Jesus came as a King in the power of the Kingdom of God, but His coat of arms was the sign of the towel. No one wanted to suppose that the long-awaited liberator would blaze the path to glory with a servant's towel for his banner, and so they were offended by it.

The religious people of Jesus' time did not take kindly to the sign of the towel. The scribes and Pharisees—very religious people, all of them—had other ideas of what religious leaders should be like. Jesus understood them well. "They make up heavy packs and pile them on men's shoulders, but will not raise a finger to lift the load themselves. Whatever they do, is done for show . . . . They like to have places of honour at feasts and the chief seats in synagogues, to be greeted respectfully in the street, and to be addressed as 'rabbi.' "[6] It was that type of person who was offended when Jesus came as a servant, and doubly offended when He demanded that His followers be servants too. Religious people want honor and respect in the community; they want to be invited to the speakers'

[4]Luke 22:27   [5]Matthew 20:28   [6]Matthew 23:4, 5, 7

table at the Rotary; they tell people to sacrifice and hardly give a dime themselves; and they want everyone to remember that they are "Reverend."

Jesus contradicted all such models of importance and influence. To those looking for places of influence in the community, His words were, "You know that in the world the recognized rulers lord it over their subjects, and make them feel the weight of authority. That is not the way with you; among you, whoever wants to be great must be your servant, and whoever wants to be first must be the willing slave of all."[7] The man who makes the towel his badge is not the man who maneuvers for a place in the power structure.

The way of the servant was His from beginning to end; it was not a mere gesture, not a once-in-a-while performance. It started in glory when He was with God. "For the divine nature was his from the first; yet he did not think to snatch at equality with God, but made himself nothing, assuming the nature of a slave."[8] He was God and became a slave. That was how it began, and that was how it ended: "Bearing the human likeness, revealed in human shape, he humbled himself, and in obedience accepted even death— death on a cross."[9] So it was all His life. His steps led Him down through servanthood to the cross.

When Jesus came as a servant, stayed as a servant, died as a servant, He was showing us what God's real excellence was like. When we hear of the glory of God, we usually think in terms of blazing majesty and unapproachable light. And that is surely part of it. But consider this. After Jesus sent Judas away from the Last Supper, away to his rendezvous with treachery, He said to the rest of the disciples: "Now the Son of Man is glorified, and in him God is glorified."[10] The glory of God was emblazoned on a towel—and on a cross!

7Mark 10:42-44   8Philippians 2:6, 7   9Philippians 2:8
10John 13:31

What is the point? The sign of the towel was not a put-on. Servanthood was not a role Jesus played on earth's stage, but His real character. And it was His character because it was God's.

Can we really grasp and be grasped by this fact? Do we still dare claim to be His followers? Would anyone know by watching us that this Servant is our Master?

2. THE SIGN OF THE TOWEL
WAS PASSED ON TO HIS BODY, THE CHURCH.

When Jesus left this earth, He passed the sign of the towel to us. We—the church—are the legitimate heirs to His strange coat of arms. This reveals our status in the world; and any Christian who is status-conscious must remember that if he is a Christian, his status is that of a servant.

Let us be realistic. We do not have a choice about whether or not to join this brotherhood of servants. If we want to be in the church, we have to be one of the servants. We are not servants just as a matter of following Jesus' example. It is not just a matter of obeying His command. There is something else, something difficult for most of us to grasp, but something nonetheless real. We are Christ's Body.

Now it is easy to turn this phrase into nothing more than a pious cliché. We can act as if being Christ's Body is only a feeling we have when we hold hands and sing "Blest Be the Tie That Binds," or the friendliness of a potluck supper in church, or the warmth of a hymn-sing. But we do not do justice to its reality that way.

We are Christ's Body, and each of us is a limb or an organ of it. Let us try to work our way into the reality behind these words. When we talked in Chapter Three about the inner essence of the community of believers, we said that our *life* is the mysterious something that surges through us and unites flesh and bones into a single organism. Our bodies express our lives.

Similarly with the Body of Christ. How does it come to be what it is? The same way as your body and mine. Christ's Body is His Body because it has His life surging through it. Christ has "become a life-giving Spirit,"[11] and the life He gives is His own. He gives it to the church, the federation of servants. We say with Paul that the life we now live is not our life, but the life which Christ lives in us.[12] "The secret is this," Paul told the church, "Christ in you, the hope of a glory to come."[13]

What does all this have to do with the sign of the towel? Simply this: Jesus left the earth and entered His Father's glory. The body that was His during thirty-odd years of servant-life on earth has left us. But in another sense He kept His body here, or He created an earthly Body through His Spirit. The church is the real presence of Christ's life on earth, making His life visible still and, what is more, *doing His work.*

Now if all this is true, it must also be true that Jesus' Body on earth still bears the sign of the towel. His way of doing His work does not change. The servant does not outrank the Master; the continuing Body is no less of a servant than the earthly Jesus was.

About three centuries after Jesus' death, the Roman emperor Constantine came conquering with a sword that had a cross carved on it. As a result, he turned the church into the respected ruling class. But the church, if it is true to the character of its inner life, comes conquering with only a towel with a cross on it. We wear the sign of the towel or we are not Christ's Body. We come as servants or we are not the representatives of the life of Jesus on earth.

Do we dare accept this disturbing reality? Do we dare be the Body of Christ? Let us look at the life of one who did.

[11] I Corinthians 15:45   [12] Galatians 2:20   [13] Colossians 1:27

3. PAUL TYPIFIED THIS KIND OF SERVANTHOOD.

"I have made myself every man's servant, to win over as many as possible."[14] Is this a fool speaking? It is, if you measure a life by the standards of a certain kind of wisdom. Paul was acquainted with that kind of wisdom—the kind that was blind to real power and glory, blind enough to crucify the Lord of glory. But Paul's words really draw the portrait of a servant.

Servants who are servants for life go to almost any length. Once he—the Right Reverend Dr. Paul—had to make his getaway by crouching inside a basket while people hoisted him over a wall. Not much churchly dignity here. But this was nothing. The portrait continues: Thirty-nine strokes with the whip—on five different occasions. Beaten with rods—three times. Stoned, shipwrecked, without sleep, without food, and much more. This was his servant's way. "All this," he says, "I do for the sake of the Gospel, to bear my part in proclaiming it."[15]

We sometimes think of Paul as some kind of superman, and perhaps we wonder if these experiences of his really matter for us. But Paul was no superman. He wanted to get rid of his "thorn in the flesh" as much as any man wants to get rid of his own. He hated to be alone in the wilderness; he hated stomach cramps from bad food; he hated to be run out of town; he hated to be hounded by his own fellow Jews. Superman myths do not account for Paul's portrait. What accounts for it is the same authentic reality that every Christian has: "the life I now live is not my life, but the life which Christ lives in me."[16] "I have strength for anything through him who gives me power."[17] Paul was no superman; he was a servant of the Lord Jesus.

There were some burdens he did not have. He did not have a hefty mortgage on a house just a little too expensive

14I Corinthians 9:19   15I Corinthians 9:22   16Galatians 2:20
17Philippians 4:13

for his budget. He did not have his status with the men at
the shop or office to worry over. He did not have that
drive to climb up the ecclesiastical ladder to a larger parish
or a more influential assignment. He did not have to
contend with an affluent society that makes men really
believe that luxuries are necessities or credit cards magic
keys to status. These burdens he did not have, and perhaps
these are heavier weights for a servant to carry than Paul's
"thorn in the flesh."

But Paul's portrait is still valid and authentic, for he was
acting as a limb of Christ's Body, conquering in the sign of
the towel.

There is one more stroke to that portrait: *freedom.*
Paul's servant life was not forced on him by circumstances.
He chose it as a free man, free from the thousands of
things that keep most of us from living the servant life.
"Have no anxiety,"[18] he once urged his fellow Christians.
In other words, do not give up the sign of the towel
because of all the things you care for. Once Paul learned
not only to accept the servant life but to choose it freely,
he had worked his mind into the mind of Christ. He had
learned that it was really true that "where the Spirit of the
Lord is, there is liberty."[19]

The sign of the towel is also the symbol of personal
freedom.

4. THE DIACONATE IS A MODEL
FOR THE SERVANT CHURCH.

If the church really is the Body of Christ, it is Christ's
visible presence in the world and servant to the world.
How does it demonstrate that this is the way it looks at
itself?

The church need not look far for ways to demonstrate

[18]Philippians 4:6   [19]II Corinthians 3:17

that it is servant. In fact, it has a ready-made way in the diaconate. Our diaconate is a structure designed to meet the same needs that led in the early church to the appointment of the Seven.[20] Very soon after Pentecost the apostles faced a crisis. Their proclamation of the Word of God left them no time to distribute food to poor people. So the church selected seven men who were "full of the Spirit" to see to it that poor people, especially widows, got enough food to eat. Now, note carefully the words with which the Acts of the Apostles concludes this account: "The word of God now spread more and more widely."[21]

Can this be a coincidence? When the church organized itself for total service—the preaching of the gospel and the care of the poor—the Word became more and more powerful. What happened was that the church altered its structure to meet a need. This alteration made the *servant* role more obvious. The Seven, especially, carried the sign of the towel for the whole church.

This role continued in the church, as is clear from the qualifications that Paul mentions for those who want to be deacons.[22] But Paul does not spell out in detail or exactly what the deacons' task was. In today's churches, the deacons tend to be managers of the church's financial affairs. They take the collections, distribute the money, keep the records, and make up the budgets. It is all quite well laid out and all rather constricted.

To the Reformed Church in the city of Geneva in the sixteenth century the deacons were the church's arm stretched out to the heart of the city, wherever human need cried for help. There was a hospital to be run. There was no Blue Cross—but there were deacons, whose job it was to see that medical care was available to all. Unemployment rose fast as refugees arrived in the city. It was the deacons' job to see that work was found for them.

[20]Read Acts 6:1-7   [21]Acts 6:7   [22]I Timothy 3:8-12

Where work was not available, they created it by building a new industry. The deacons waged Geneva's War on Poverty. They raised the money to care for the needy in the city. They arranged for new trades to be learned by young men out of work. In brief, wherever there was human need, the deacons of the church were organized to do something about it. In Calvin's Geneva, the church's deacons were the servants of all men; and through the deacons so was the church.

The diaconate, then, is the organizational way of accepting from Jesus His sign of the towel, the symbol of servanthood. But two things have to be remembered here: First, the whole church is a diaconate. For practical reasons, some of the servant's task is done by deacons. But Jesus' whole life was spent in service, and this is what He asks of *all* who follow Him. Diaconate spells out the whole character, the full spirit, and the great purpose of the church's mission to the world. The Body of Christ is not a loose bundle of separated functions. The whole Body is involved in the service. And the official deacons have the right to tap the talents and resources of every member. For we are all limbs of one Body.

Second, we must ask whether modern deacons really do stand for service to the world. Or do they stand as earnest guardians of the balanced budget, representative of the church's concern to get its own comforts secured and its own financial house in order? The world outside notices those churches whose properties are very valuable and whose income from them escapes even secular taxation. But it notices as well the way the church ignores human need at its doorsteps. How the churches recoiled when black leaders talked about reparation payments to make up for church-supported injustice to black people in the history of Christianized America. How different things would be if these black leaders could point to the church's diaconate as the single hand that fed the poor, the single mouth that cried out for justice, and the single heart that bled for the oppressed.

This is a time when every church must examine itself. Is it a church whose every member is a deacon? Is it a church whose official elected deacons—who only represent all the deacons—are really Jesus' servants to their communities?

B. GLORY IS ONLY FOR THOSE WHO SUFFER.

In Paul's great chapter on victory and comfort, Romans 8, he promises that nothing will separate us from God's love in Christ. All things work out well for those who are called according to God's purpose. But Paul also spells out the condition: suffering with Christ. "We are God's heirs and Christ's fellow-heirs, if we share his sufferings now . . . ."[1] There it is, written plain for every Christian who cherishes the hope of glory. Glory is only for those who suffer.

What does this say to a generation whose biggest preoccupation is avoiding pain? The whole world today is engineered to help us escape suffering. Our age boasts of its greatest achievement as escape from drudgery. Pain pills of various sorts are the biggest buyers of commercial time on television. We are running hard to get away from suffering. The escape is not always as routine as swallowing pills. More subtle, but more dangerous, is refusal to get involved: our escape from other people's hurts. A crowd watches a girl being attacked, and no one responds. How typical of our time. Don't get involved, because if you do, you might get hurt too.

Now to Christian people, living in a world determined by all means to keep away from pain, comes the word: there is no glory without suffering. Can we digest that truth?

[1] Romans 8:17

Before we proceed, we should look at what this truth does *not* mean. First of all, not just any pain will qualify. Our suffering must be suffering *with Christ.* Not every migraine headache, not even every malignant cancer, will qualify us for glory. The suffering Paul is referring to must be Christ's own suffering.

Furthermore, we must not pervert Paul's words into something sick. We are not called to enjoy suffering or to look for it. That would be morbid, and it would not be Jesus' way. Jesus took no delight in His suffering. The man in the Garden of Gethsemane was not one enjoying the terrible prospect of Calvary. He was sweating it out in blood. He prayed in fear and trembling for the cup to be taken away—if it could be His Father's will. Suffering with Christ—even as the necessary condition for reigning with Him—is not the same as a sick masochism.

Finally, suffering is not always identical to physical pain. A soldier in wartime might break his ankle the night before his company is to go out on a very dangerous mission. His ankle would hurt, but he would not be suffering. On the other hand, there is terrible suffering that involves no physical pain at all. A father who discovers his daughter is on drugs suffers in a way that no medicine can reach. Suffering is bigger than pain. Our Lord's suffering bears this out. The nails of the cross tore His flesh, but His deepest hurt He expressed this way: "My God, my God, why hast thou forsaken me?"[2]

Since we must suffer with Jesus, we must ask what Jesus' style of suffering was. His whole life, from birth to death, was styled by suffering. What made Him suffer? The answer is *people.* The needs, the tragedies, the pains, the suffering, as well as the resistance of people made Him suffer.

Jesus was involved. He was God's own way of getting at

2Matthew 27:46

our sin and misery. We were caught as captives of the law of sin and death, and Jesus got inside our life on earth—not as a tourist sightseeing, but as a citizen of our world. This is what incarnation means. Once He was totally involved, He was vulnerable, open to hurts. And since He was really involved where suffering is epidemic, He was hurt.

Jesus did not hurt only when people savagely struck Him or when they reviled Him. He hurt *with* people. He wept when others suffered.[3] He suffered because He was involved, deeply and personally, in their suffering lives.

But Jesus did not only suffer with people; He suffered *for* them. His was the work of atonement. "On himself he bore our sufferings, our torments he endured . . . . He was pierced for our transgressions, tortured for our in-iquities . . . , stricken to the death for my people's trans-gression."[4] He suffered for us as well as with us. This is our last and only recourse. What He did for us need never and can never be done again. In this His suffering is finished. "We have been consecrated, through the offering of the body of Jesus Christ once for all."[5]

Some Christians have used this "once for all" clause as an escape from suffering. They see Jesus' precious blood, shed for us, as an invitation to a life of spiritual luxury: the cross was Christ's, the happiness and ease of eternal security are ours. But read Paul once more: "God's heirs and Christ's fellow-heirs *if we share his suffering.*"

"Once for all"—and yet, in another sense, not finished. Paul makes it clear to the Christians at Colossae. "It is now my happiness to suffer for you. This is my way of helping to complete, in my poor human flesh, the full tale of Christ's affliction still to be endured, for the sake of his body which is the church."[6] Paul suffers for the sake of Christ's Body; in other words, as a limb of that Body. His

[3]Read John 11:35   [4]Isaiah 53:4, 5, 8   [5]Hebrews 10:10
[6]Colossians 1:24

suffering carries on the suffering of Jesus, which goes on, through the world, for the needs of men everywhere. Christ's suffering goes on because His Body suffers. And if it does not suffer, it is not His Body. We see, then, that suffering is not only a condition for glory but also the inevitable result of being Christ's Body.

Jesus Christ was involved with real people in a real world of suffering. He was vulnerable because He was involved; and being vulnerable in our kind of suffering world, He suffered all His life long. His Body follows the same route through the world, becoming involved with real people in their real suffering. To the extent that it is involved, it is vulnerable; and being vulnerable, it gets hurt.

Are we willing to be the Body of Christ? Are we ready to take Jesus' route through the world? Does the church want to take only one aspect of Jesus' life as its own: the few times of rest He took in the living room of Martha and Mary? Is this not the case with many churches in the suburbs—they want only rest and recreation on the sidelines of the city where they can wait out the crises of our day?

Think about it. Is the white church ready to be so wholly involved with suffering black people that it becomes vulnerable to their wounds? Is the white church able, with Jesus, to feel inside its heart the sufferings that black people have endured? That takes a lot of heart, but only as the church is somehow with those who suffer can it suffer too.

Suffering and mission are tied up together. Christ's mission was to die for the world, and He fulfilled that mission. So the church need not suffer to atone for sins. It does not suffer to reconcile the world; it suffers when it is God's minister of reconciliation to the world.

Without suffering there is usually only the feeblest gesture at mission. The call to suffering includes suffering *with;* wherever people are hurting, wherever people are lost, wherever people are victims of war, injustice, inhumanity, the church suffers with them. And unless it suffers with, it cannot witness to people.

C. IT IS DIFFICULT FOR THE CHURCH TO BE TRUE TO ITS WORDS ABOUT SERVANTHOOD.

We live and work under the sign of the towel. But there are all sorts of ways we can deny what the towel signifies. Integrity does not come easy in any part of life; it is hardest of all to be true to the words we use about servanthood. Let us look at three of the routes we use to escape their force.

1. THE CHURCH MAY ESCAPE SERVANTHOOD BY SERVING ITS OWN ESTABLISHMENT.

We saw in Chapter Five that the Spirit is a friend of organization. Wherever the life of the Spirit emerges, it becomes organized for service. But organizations sometimes become ends in themselves. Whenever new threats or new challenges appear, we become uneasy about the organization, and we turn inward to find ways to shore it up and keep it secure. Once this happens, the organization becomes the establishment. An establishment is an institution that once served the world and now serves itself.

It is not difficult to detect an organization that has started turning into an establishment. People become fidgety about changes going on. They want the jargon to stay the same, worried that a new vocabulary might signal a new message. They want the liturgy intact, comfortable as an old shoe. They want the preacher to keep his dignity, and not be lowered beneath his station by hobnobbing with long-haired, shoeless outsiders. They want the budget balanced, the mortgage paid off on schedule. They want the ship to be floating smoothly. And what they do not want is to think that everything about the church—including the budget, the liturgy, the vocabulary—has to be geared for service.

Working at keeping the establishment safe *is* hard work—and it looks like service. But it may be only institutional self-service. And it may be an escape from Christ's summons to be His suffering servant in our suffering world.

2. A CONGREGATION MAY AVOID SERVICE BY SEEING ITS CHURCH AS A FORTRESS.

A church member once asked a visitor what he thought of a new sanctuary. "I think it would make a fine fortress," came the answer.

A fortress? Yes, it would be very hard for vandals to break in. The doors are heavy, and locked most of the time. And, in their own way, the people are locked into it, not by the doors, literally, but by other things. Congregations "liberated from the law of sin and death" often go into bondage again—to their mortgage. The preacher is bound too. His prophetic voice is toned down and fenced in. He dare not upset the people who want most of all to secure the fort. They are too easily disturbed; and when they are disturbed they may withhold their money from the budget. So the preacher walks with care; no radical, prophetic words. And this gets to be his style: almost unconsciously he tunes his message to the mortgage.

New programs that demand a shift in budget priorities? New services? How can a congregation begin them when it is burdened with the task of holding the fort? And so it tries to escape from service.

3. ORTHODOXY MAY BE USED AS AN ESCAPE FROM SERVICE.

The orthodox church knows where the real issues of truth are. It knows the pitfalls of the social gospel. It knows about the risks of mission and the heresy of free will and mass evangelism. This is its strength. Its weakness is that it sometimes uses these superior insights as an escape hatch from service.

When the Word comes to be a servant to the whole world in all its needs, it can easily be translated as social gospel. When the Word comes to send the church into mission to the world, it can easily be translated as a fundamentalist heresy. But when we use the orthodox sensitivity for sniffing out heresy as a refuge from service, we deny our Lord's own will. When we transform our duty to keep the faith into an inner-directed urge to avoid suffering in the world, we are using it as an escape route from service.

Let us be honest. The institution does need tending. The building does need paying for. The faith does need keeping. But none of these will allow us, in the eyes of the Lord, to escape from servanthood. The sign of the towel tells us still: the church of Jesus Christ is His servant in our world.

D. THE WAY OF A SERVANT IS THE WAY OF JOY.

This chapter will have been completely wasted if it seems to say that the Christian life is nothing but bitter suffering and homeless servitude. What we said about celebration still holds true: the keynote of the Body of Christ is joy.

The church knows that the last word about life is not the sordid headlines of every night's newspaper, nor the weary undertones of defeat in the heart of the city, nor the pathos of a new generation vainly trying to create another world to replace the one it rejects. The last word is Victory. "We have his promise, and look forward to new heavens and a new earth."[1]

[1] II Peter 3:13

The route is from celebration to involvement; from victory to service; from joy to vulnerability. The church does not grasp desperately for joy out of a morass of morbidity, but plunges gladly into service from the platform of hope.

The servant style is not a posture of weakness. It comes from insight into the power and the glory of God. A strange power, which looks to some like weakness, comes from service given by the suffering servant. Christ crucified—the weakness of God—turned the powers of the world on their heads. This is the style that the church maintains.

It comes from a vision of glory. Servants do not look glorious to most people, and suffering servants even less so. But we must let the glorious God provide the right idea of what real glory is. The glory of God was revealed to human eyes when a servant, with visage marred, was left hanging to die on tree. The glory of God was set on display when a man came to us, serving all men all the way.

* * *

There it is—the power and the glory, the victory and the hope. Out of these resources we can dare to be suffering servants to the world. The style was set by Jesus, so we will never be out of style in servant's garb. He supplies the resources of His powerful grace all along the route. Will we go along with Him under the sign of the towel?

CHAPTER SEVEN

Moving Out on the Way

The church on the move in mission to the world is not a church that sends out a few missionaries, but a whole church that is sent. A church in mission is a church moving out, from the center to the fringes, from the sanctuary to the marketplaces, from the hearing of God's Word to the doing of God's work. Is this a description of your church and mine?

Missions is always a two-way street. The church is inviting people in to hear, to believe, to obey, and to live the good news: that is one side—bringing in. But there is an outward direction too. Missions summons the church to follow its Lord outside the stained-glass refuge into the world of hurting people and lost souls. Missions has these two aspects—bringing in and going out. The church is *both* "Ark" and "Exodus."

"I am the door," Jesus said, "anyone who comes into the fold through me shall be safe. He shall *go in and out* and shall find pasturage."[1] This points us to a key concept. Whatever else the church does in response to the needs of the people around it, the single gift it brings is the message about Jesus Christ, doorway to the new life. But He is both the doorway in to salvation and the doorway out to service, in to security from the ravages of guilt and out to the risks of service to the suffering, in to the

[1] John 10:9

sheepfold and out to the fields. One door, which swings two ways.

A. THE CHURCH IS SUMMONED TO FOLLOW THE LORD OUT INTO THE WORLD.

1. THE CHURCH MUST MINISTER TO ALL THE PEOPLE OF THE WORLD.

> From Greenland's icy mountains,
> From India's coral strand,
> Where Afric's sunny fountains
> Roll down their golden sand . . . .

That familiar hymn, with its broad vision, was written in 1823. In the century and a half since then, the field has become complicated beyond the wildest dreams of any churchman of that day. Then the biggest obstacle was "getting there." Now getting there is easy. It is what is there and who is there that staggers us.

Take the matter of sheer numbers. When "From Greenland's Icy Mountains" first stirred the missionary imagination, the population of the world had been doubling once every two thousand years or so—a steady but slow growth. In approximately a hundred years following the writing of the hymn, the world's population doubled again. Now it is doubling approximately every thirty-five years. When space travelers looked at the planet earth from the moon in 1968, they saw a globe with three-and-a-half billion people on it. Since then, about a million more have been arriving every week. Experts are wondering aloud, in panic, how many more the earth can sustain. The church may well wonder how it can bring the Bread of Life to that many.

Most versions of that missionary hymn end the first stanza with the words: "They call us to deliver / their lands from error's chain." That is certainly not true today, if it ever was. *They* call for agricultural experts, for commercial investors, for war machinery. They do not call for missionaries. In the past, missionaries were welcomed as the van of imperialist colonizers. Today neither the missionaries nor the colonizers are wanted. Another version of the hymn changes the line—more biblically and realistically—to "*Christ* calls us to deliver. . . ."

2. THE WORLD TO WHICH THE CHURCH MINISTERS IS CHANGING.

The population explosion is only the most obvious and statistical side of the challenge. It is not the number of people but the quality of life that is the greatest challenge. The shape of human life is changing. The quality of life is deteriorating spiritually. And the church must embrace in love, not a lost world of yesterday, but the lost world of today and tomorrow.

We shall mention only a few facets here. Technology, for one thing, is changing life and profoundly changing man with it. In the garden long ago, man was given a mandate by God to subdue nature. Now man is becoming part of the nature that is being subdued. Man is being changed to a thing that can be manipulated and controlled and made happy by technology. Pills can change a man who is uptight and unbearable to one who is docile and likeable. What does the future hold? Through what is called *cloning*, scientists are working on ways of producing exact duplicates of any person we happen to like. If you want your future son to be exactly like your favorite hero, it will be possible to arrange that through genetic manipulation. If a labor union strikes, threatening a national emergency, we may be able to put chemicals in the drinking water of union members, and make them more than happy to go back to work.

Technology is rushing us into a strange and possibly dehumanizing future. It provides innumerable gadgets for us to enjoy, reduces our working hours to give us time to enjoy them, but in the end may reduce us precisely to that—gadget enjoyers and gadget disposers.

a. Life today is increasingly urbanized.

A prominent feature of changing life is the city. Like it or not, we are all becoming citified, and the church is creeping into that city with a structure meant for the village. City life changes people profoundly. It makes them mobile; one-third of Los Angeles County, for example, is now paved over with concrete for automobiles. Not only do people move about from home to every place imaginable, they also move from home to home. Between March 1967 and March 1968, more than 36 million Americans changed their place of residence. Industry executives are moved about like pawns on chessboards; but people in all levels of society are becoming nomads. Since 1948 every year has seen one family out of five change its residence.

b. The family is breaking down.

In the face of all this, the support of the family is disappearing. Friends and neighbors used to help keep families together. Today people are strangers in their own neighborhood, and their friends are only casual. Families used to have their roots nourished by their faith—or at least by their church; but now, increasingly, they pull up their spiritual roots when they pull up stakes to move. Pills are closer at hand than God. The mystique of birth and death was once something real to children, binding them deep in their minds to the mysteries of family beginnings and endings. That mystique is now gone. Babies, born in the hospital, are merely brought home to compete for a diminishing supply of parental affection. Grandparents do not really die, in the old sense; they merely vanish from the old people's home, where children never like to visit anyway. Families are fractured as much by the changes in the quality of life as by the immoral decisions that parents make.

It is not only the fact that husbands and wives ignore what they once accepted as a vow "till death do us part" that breaks up families. The generation gap between parents and their offspring is a divisive force. Parents' insane chase for "the good life" has disenchanted youth. They are rejecting their parent's plastic society and the veneer of morals they coated it with. The youth are rejecting both the superficiality of suburban culture and the immorality of suburban hypocrisy, and in that sense are rejecting the world and life of their parents. Most of all, however, parents and offspring are separated because our children were born into a world that is changing with jet-age speed. The family is being fractured because the world of the present is fractured from the world of the past.

c. Traditional morality has lost its hold on man.

Meanwhile, we have moved into a post-moral age. Once people who no longer believed in God still believed in moral law. There was a right and wrong, they thought, even if there was no God who made things right or wrong. Now, the very concept of right and wrong has become obsolete for many. For parents, what is "right" is what brings the greatest amount of security and success. For youth, recognizing the emptiness of this, there is a new definition: what is "right" is what brings freedom; what is wrong is what makes one a slave of a system, any system. What makes one feel good? What does not get in the way of personal satisfaction? What do feelings desire? What does freedom demand? These are the important questions for the post-moral mind.

Along with a post-moral mind comes a "mirror complex." Futurists predict that as we go along, people are going to become mirror gazers, obsessed with what they *look* like, rather than what they *are* like. Dress, cosmetics, and drugs of all sorts that promise a good image, will be the "best buys" of the future.

More than 1500 years ago St. Augustine said: "Thou hast created us for Thyself, and our heart is not quiet until it rests in Thee." Modern man is demonstrating that. We have pills for everything except the soul. Is this perhaps the deepest explanation for the drug craze—not simply a sensual desire for kicks, but a deep religious desire for peace? Is this the "why" of astrology, of spiritualist cults, of communes? The church must find out.

3. THE CHURCH MUST CONFRONT UNJUST SOCIAL STRUCTURES.

There is one more item on the agenda of need and hurt: social structures that foster injustice. We shall mention only one facet of it—the racial crisis. Without a doubt, the greatest moral burden of North America is its treatment of its minority races.

Here, too, the picture has changed. Once it seemed that all that was needed was to convert the hearts of people to love the black person. If we learned to love our black neighbors, the problem would be solved, because we would then open our shops, our schools, our churches, and our neighborhoods to them, and they would join us in an equal society. Now we know better. In the first place, the hearts of people have not been changed, and their shops, schools, churches, and neighborhoods are not open. But even if they had been, the enormity of the problem would be lessened only slightly.

We have discovered that blacks are caught, not only in the clutches of personal prejudice, but in a huge network of social structures that pin them down in injustice. They are caught in the city. In 1910, 73 percent of black people in this country lived in rural areas; in 1960, 73 percent of them lived in the large cities, and that number is growing. Furthermore, they live in the center of the cities, the old, dilapidated, unfit center that we call the ghetto. All the unsolved problems of the city are dumped on the black population as genteel whites flee to the fringes of the city.

There are numerous other sides to the oppression of blacks. A bad tax structure condemns the poor man who owns a small house to a far larger payment of taxes, proportionately, than the middle-class white man. An obsolete court system puts a black man in jail faster and keeps him there longer than it does white men. Middle- and upper-class whites know how and are financially able to hire lawyers; and "getting a lawyer" is the name of the game if you want to keep yourself or your children out of jail. Technology has encouraged industry; and taxes have pressed it to move away from the city, where blacks live. So industry takes its clean new machines, sets them in clean new buildings out in clean new suburbs, and leaves the black man behind without a job. Add all of these contemporary forces to what has been going on for a century—breaking down of the black family, pestilent prejudice, and inculcation of a sense of inferiority—and you have a worse racial situation than there was twenty-odd years ago.

B. THE CHURCH THAT FOLLOWS THE LORD HAS A DEMANDING TASK.

All in all, the church that seeks, by the power of God's love, to embrace the bleeding city to itself has a titanic task. But God's calling to the church is for today's needs, not yesterday's, for this world, not a fantasy world. In our dreams and visions of tomorrow we must not lose sight of our very real world as it is today. Is it less than reasonable to call ourselves to self-examination: to appraise our life style, our faith, our resources, and our hopes? Is it not reasonable that we re-examine the will of God in Christ for us today?

The Bible, we read, was inspired by God for this purpose: "that the man who belongs to God may be efficient and equipped for good work of every kind."[1] Good works are works that grow out of—but do not earn—grace. Where there are no good works, there is no grace.

Cheap grace has no place in God's enterprise. Grace cost God His Son. Grace, given freely, demands the discipline of radical discipleship. Grace breeds manly Christians, zealous for God's justice; and it breeds joy for God's love. Let us look at some of the qualities of grace that our mission to the world requires.

1. MEN OF GOD MUST BE LOYAL TO CHRIST.

A decisive issue is "single-hearted devotion to Christ."[2] Loyalty is the primary quality of the man of God for our time. The servant of the Suffering Servant is the man or woman who admits Him as Master. Every person must be loyal to something; for no man's heart is big enough to survive devotion to itself. Man needs something bigger than himself, some transcendent cause or some transcendent ideal, or, if he is blessed, some transcendent Person. Persons committed in loyalty to Christ are loyal to the only one great enough to deserve ultimate loyalty, and the only one who can be trusted to employ that loyalty for blessing. Persons loyal to Christ are loyal servants for Christ.

[1] II Timothy 3:17   [2] II Corinthians 11:3

The world today is looking for something to be loyal to. Too often people let loyalty shrink to little individuals like themselves. They will listen to calls for a better commitment. But they demand—as a condition for listening—a church that demonstrates that it is in deed, and not just in word, loyal to the Friend of sinners, to the Suffering Servant who came not to be served but to serve. Will they recognize this loyalty in our church?

Loyalty to Christ does not mean loyalty to a social ideal, a reforming crusade, or a political cause. The church's loyalty is not to progress or happiness or social schemes. The church is neither liberal nor conservative; it is ally neither of the Americans for Democratic Action nor the John Birch Society. It is loyal to Jesus Christ, and for His sake and the sake of His gospel it moves out to modern man as he cries out for help.

2. MEN OF GOD ARE MEN OF COMPASSION.

The *religious* man is usually a person with a natural instinct for law and order; the *man of God* is a person compelled by God's love to have compassion for needy people. The religious man looks at the city with fear and distrust. He sees the city in terms of law enforcement and law breaking, of power structures and political ineptness. The man of God sees the city in terms of all these too, but he sees it first of all in terms of *people*. The religious man imitates the insecure style of the world; he uses his religion only to bolster his own ego. The man of God imitates the secure style of the outgoing, self-giving, compassionate God.

God's compassion for the city—a compassion that religious Jonah could not swallow—is our guide. Jonah suspected that God was soft on law and order and too easy on violent folk. "I knew that thou art 'a god gracious and compassionate, long-suffering and ever constant, and always willing to repent of the disaster.' "[3] This is why he had fled to Tarshish. Jonah hated the violent city Nineveh and wanted God to destroy it. God felt differently, and spared the city. Then came the vine to give shade to the frustrated prophet, and the worm to destroy the vine. Jonah felt something: blind, destructive anger, an anger so wild that it filled Jonah with a wish for death. But he felt it, and that was God's object lesson: "You are sorry for the gourd, though you did not have the trouble of growing it, a plant which came up in a night and withered in a night. And should not I be sorry for the great city of Nineveh, with its hundred and twenty thousand who cannot tell their right hand from their left, and cattle without number?"[4]

God's compassion for the violent city, born of a vision of the city as people, souls, human beings, led Him to hold the city in His arms. The religious man had to learn what it meant to be a man of God.

What about compassion for our city? Do we have compassion for the children of the city? No one asked them where they preferred to be born. No one asked whether they wanted to be born into a world of dirt, disorder, and distortion of human values. Born into a situation that would send us running in horror if we but visited it for a day, they are led by advertising to believe that the world is theirs for the flash of a credit card. They are led to nourish expectations that are doomed to be frustrated. The man of God has compassion on the children of the city because God has compassion.

Jesus often mirrored this quality of God. "The sight of the people moved him to pity."[5] "He saw a great crowd; his heart went out to them."[6] He told His disciples, "I feel sorry for all these people; they . . . have nothing to eat."[7]

[3]Jonah 4:2   [4]Jonah 4:10, 11   [5]Matthew 9:36
[6]Matthew 14:14   [7]Matthew 15:32

Again and again, in all four Gospel records, the theme is the compassion of Jesus. No wonder, then, that when He looked at the city from a hilltop, He wept. If Jesus' life is distinguished by compassion, what about anyone who calls himself the brother of Jesus?

Compassion solves no problems. It does not provide the church with solutions to social ills. But without compassion there is no real solution to any human problem confronting man and the church. Compassion is not enough, but nothing is enough without compassion.

3. MEN OF GOD ARE CONSUMED WITH A PASSION FOR GOD'S JUSTICE.

Justice demands that things be kept secure and equitable. God is, without question, the God of justice. "He it is who will judge the world with justice."[8] "Can mortal man be more righteous than God?"[9] The answer is obvious. "There is no god but me; there is no god other than I, victorious and able to save."[10] The man of God seeks justice because his God is the perfect example of true justice.

Justice is not just a matter of words. We have to find their meaning; and the man of God wants biblical meanings for biblical words. Justice takes on its own colors and shapes in the Word of God, and we must let that Word paint those colors and create those shapes.

We take our cue from salvation by faith alone. Paul calls it justification by grace through faith. When a man is justified by God, he must be *justly* justified. The Pharisee thought he knew what this meant: God was just in the sense that He called a spade a spade, and that was the end of it. If a man is right God rewards him; if he is wrong, He punishes him. In other words, He rewards men according

[8]Psalm 9:8   [9]Job 4:17   [10]Isaiah 45:21

to their merit, and merit is earned by obedience to the moral law. That, and that only, is God's *justice.*

Compare that with Paul's revolutionary words about justice. "Now, quite independently of law, God's justice has been brought to light .... For all alike have sinned, and are deprived of the divine splendour, and all are justified by God's free grace alone .... God meant by this to demonstrate his justice ... showing that he is himself just and also justifies any man who puts his faith in Jesus."[11]

Reflect on these words for a moment. God is just, and He shows His justice by being gracious to sinners. We must not let this point slide by. God does not forget justice when He remembers mercy. He is just in showing mercy. He deals with sinful people according to their needs, not according to their merits, because He loves—enough to provide His only Son for their salvation. This is God's justice, the divine justice that turned the world upside down.

What Paul said was not really new. The Pharisees had long forgotten it, but the prophets had much earlier proclaimed the same message from God. Out of their concern for people's needs, they cried for justice in the land. The words of Amos are especially powerful: "Let justice roll on like a river and righteousness like an ever-flowing stream."[12]

This justice that the prophets had in mind was not merely the justice that is represented by the blindfolded goddess of justice balancing the scales. The prophets were thinking of needs, human needs, suffered by the poor and dispossessed. When they cried for the people to care for the widow, the orphan, the poor, and the stranger, they were crying for justice. Israel was not being asked for charity and benevolence to the poor. To feed the poor and

11Romans 3:21, 23-26   12Amos 5:24

to care for the widow was *justice.* When God cares for the weak and the distressed, it is a concern, not for charity, but for justice. Justice and mercy are one. For God's way of justice is to deal with men according to their needs. [13] The way of God is not the charitable handout, but the way of justice. Listen to a few of the prophets:

Isaiah: "The Lord opens the indictment against the elders of his people and their officers: You have ravaged the vineyard, and the spoils of the poor are in your houses." [14]

Jeremiah: "Deal justly and fairly, rescue the victim from his oppressor, do not ill-treat or do violence to the alien, the orphan or the widow." [15]

Zechariah: "Administer true justice, show loyalty and compassion to one another, do not oppress the orphan and the widow, the alien and the poor." [16]

The man of God is the man consumed with passion for God's kind of justice. When he sees people left out of society's goods, oppressed by injustice, exploited by avarice, and dehumanized by a brutal welfare system, he is aroused to call anew for justice—not according to merits of good works, but according to the pressure of human need.

The church of Christ is the gathering of those who have experienced the taste of God's wonderful kind of justice. They are the first to admit that they have been dealt with not according to their merit, but according to God's grace. And this is justice—of God's sort. How can they not respond to human need in our time by reflecting the same strange justice of their forgiving God? The man of God is a man of justice—God's kind of justice!

[13]Read Exodus 22:21-25 [14]Isaiah 3:14 [15]Jeremiah 22:3
[16]Zechariah 7:9, 10

C. AS IT MOVES OUT INTO THE WORLD, THE CHURCH'S DEEDS MUST BE CONSISTENT WITH ITS WORDS.

Credibility is one of the major issues of our time. Are the leaders of our government credible? Do they back up their words with consistent action? Are the claims made by advertisers reliable? Seldom have such questions been as prominent as they are today. But the church is in the crucible too. All sorts of people, from ministers to young rebels, are making new demands that the church of Christ be more credible. And the standard of credibility is consistency between words and deeds.

1. JESUS SET THE PATTERN.

Jesus taught and acted. What He did was a demonstration of what He said. He proclaimed the coming of the Kingdom of God and did the kind of things that must happen when the Kingdom of God comes in power.

When He encountered hunger, He acted to give people something to eat.[1] When He met people possessed, He sent the demons out.[2] When He met blind people, He made them see.[3] When He encountered people who were paralyzed, He made them walk.[4] These are just a few examples of one prevailing fact: where Jesus saw a need, He moved out toward it and met it.

Jesus did not demand a trial period for needy people. He did not wait until they proved themselves worthy. He did not postpone action until He could guarantee gratitude or faith. He did not set up qualifications. The condition was need; the inner resources were His power; the motivation was His compassion.

[1]Read John 6:1-13   [2]Read Luke 8:26-39   [3]Read John 9:1-12
[4]Mark 2:1-12

Nor did Jesus use His acts as a gimmick to attract attention. The needs of men were His concern, and His miracles of healing demonstrated the kind of total Savior He was and is.

Needless to say, His actions never made His message unnecessary. He proclaimed the *one* way into the Kingdom. He preached the coming of God's Kingdom, not man's—a Kingdom that came, not by works of human reform, but by the act of divine atonement. His words made plain what His acts were all about, where they came from, and what they were for. But neither did He ever separate the Word from the act. The acts demonstrated the validity of the Word: the Word illuminated the meaning of the acts. When John the Baptist quivered with doubt, and sent friends to get a clear word from Jesus on His identity, Jesus said: "Go and tell John what you hear and see: the blind recover their sight, the lame walk, the lepers are made clean, the deaf hear, the dead are raised to life, the poor are hearing the good news."[5] Jesus' message to John is clear. You can believe Me because of what your disciples hear and see, the word and the deed. This is prophetic credibility.

2. HE EXPECTS US TO FOLLOW HIS PATTERN.

Can we keep the coupling of word and deed intact? How often we immobilize ourselves by debating our priorities. Jesus moved His disciples out to "proclaim the kingdom and to heal."[6] Once again, the familiar combination: speak and do; word and act; preach the message of the Kingdom and perform the deeds of the Kingdom.

Credibility before men demands action. But so does credibility before God. When men are exposed before His judgment, they will be asked surprising questions—like

[5]Matthew 11:4, 5   [6]Luke 9:2

what they did for the seamy folk locked up in the city jail. Are we prepared to take Jesus' words about the judgment as seriously as He meant them? "Then the king will say to those on his right hand, 'You have my Father's blessing; come, enter and possess the kingdom that has been ready for you since the world was made. For when I was hungry, you gave me food; when thirsty, you gave me drink; when I was a stranger you took me into your home, when naked you clothed me; when I was ill you came to my help, when in prison you visited me."[7]

Several profound realities are expressed in these words. First, there is Jesus' identification of Himself with all sorts of people in all sorts of trouble. Second, the judgment is based on what those before the throne *did*. But another facet is not to be overlooked. When those who had not done anything were judged and rejected, they were amazed.[8] Their calloused souls never recognized the troubled people around them and never discerned that those around them who were suffering represented Jesus Himself. In effect they were saying, "If we had only known it was you, we would have done something." What Jesus wanted, however, was for them to act simply on the basis of the need of the people at hand.

The disciple does not base his action on a neat calculation. He does not act because he wants to come out favorably at the judgment. He does not act because of Jesus' identity with the poor. He moves out to act as Jesus acted: because the need is out there and the love of God is within.

So the pattern for us is parallel to that set by Jesus. Word and deed must be joined. There is no way to "possess the mind of Christ"[9] without embracing the world as He did. Christian people cannot proclaim mercy

[7]Matthew 25:34-36   [8]Matthew 25:44   [9]I Corinthians 2:16

without doing mercy or preach justice without acting justly and seeking justice—in the biblical sense.

The word without the action is empty; the deed without the word is ambiguous. The church has to be able to answer modern doubters with the same kind of word that Jesus sent back to John the Baptist.

But what of the question of priority? Granted both word and action are needed, does not one come first in importance? There *is* a priority here, but woe to the church that uses the priority of one as an excuse to leave the other alone. What has priority is the salvation that God gave us in Christ. In that sense the message of what God has done has priority over the deeds that we do. Paul speaks to this: "For the grace of God has dawned upon the world with healing for all mankind."[10] This comes to man as the prior fact. But Paul goes on to speak of our response to God's salvation. By this grace of God "we are disciplined . . . to live a life of temperance, honesty, and godliness in the present age."[11]

God has priority, and the message of His grace has priority. But the actions that go along with the message are necessary to make the messengers of His salvation credible to the world.

D. THE CHURCH MUST BE A TRUSTWORTHY STEWARD OF ITS OPPORTUNITIES.

"Stewards are expected to show themselves trustworthy."[1] That is the test of good stewardship. Not every congregation can do everything, but every person and every congregation is expected to be a good steward of what opportunities they have to do something.

Jesus told a familiar parable that makes this point. A servant was entrusted by his master with a single bag of

[10]Titus 2:11   [11]Titus 2:12   [1]I Corinthians 4:2

gold, less than either of his master's other two servants were given. But instead of employing the gold in business and making a profit, as the others did, the servant with one bag hid it for safe-keeping. The master's word to him was: "You lazy rascal."[2] He was a bad steward of the single opportunity he had.

Every congregation has a neighborhood around it, and every neighborhood has people who are hurting, people who are lonely, people who may be lost. Every church is located in a community, and every community has its jail, its poor people, its suffering people. So every congregation is the steward of an opportunity. All that is expected of stewards is that they be trustworthy in that opportunity.

Congregations sometimes fail to perceive the full resources they have to be good stewards. Consider the retired. Shelved before their time by competitive industry, they are often shelved before God's time by the church. Or think of the potential for the church as its members in automated industries have shorter workweeks. The talents and energy of the deacons of the church have often been ridiculously underemployed. Let deacons be the servants of God to the congregation—stubbornly tapping resources people did not even know they had. Let deacons be the servants of God to the world's needy at a time when society's welfare program is crumbling from over-taxation and inhumanity to its recipients. Let the deacons, planning imaginatively together, give biblically inspired guidance to future plans for guaranteed annual incomes.

Lester De Koster has suggested this prophetic possibility: "What if the nation's answer to welfare becomes a guaranteed annual income? . . . What if it happens? . . . *Who* will counsel right use of such income? Just the overloaded caseworker? *Who* will fend off the loan shark's thirty percent interest? Who will teach buying skills, shop-

---

[2]Matthew 25:14-30

ping habits, brand discrimination, package labels, etc., etc.—in short, just plain good stewardship? *We* could . . . . Come, deacons, and all who share diaconal concern for the neighbor—and that *ought* to be all of us—there is a form of 'witness' that will open its doors . . . and it is one form of that love *in-deed* without which all our words clink and clank. . . . We have the funds, if we allocate them for it, to hire professional, Christian, social workers; to set up professionally designed counseling centers with radii reaching into the homes of the poor; and we have the schools to train such 'deacons' and 'deaconesses.' " This is but one example of how imaginative use of neglected resources might help the congregation be a better steward. Times change, and as they change they create new opportunities for stewardship.

All that the Lord requires of stewards is that they be trustworthy, each according to his opportunity.

E. THE CHURCH MOVES OUT IN STRENGTH.

The church does not move out in mission by tagging along behind the world's power structures. The church moves out in strength—a disguised strength, like God's power at Calvary, shaped like what man would call weakness. This is a basic and permanent fact about the church that many churches have forgotten and keep forgetting. Some forget it and try to come on with the trappings of worldly power. Others forget it and mistake their own disguised strength as weakness, never daring to move out. But the church moves out, in fact, with almost incredible strength.

The church, made up of very puny people, moved out only after victory was won. *Jesus is Lord*—this is the basic fact of the church's faith and existence. Jesus Christ led captivity captive, disarmed the powers of the air, and broke the back of the forces that had enslaved human history in defeat, frustration, and imminent chaos. We move out in strength because He has overcome.

The victory of Jesus Christ at Easter tells us something about the character of the struggle we face. Paul tells us plainly: "Our fight is not against human foes, but against cosmic powers, against the authorities and potentates of this dark world, against the superhuman forces of evil in the heavens."[1] Christ's victory notwithstanding, we are still fighting, for the powers have a way of postponing their final debacle, shaking their fist hard in the teeth of defeat. Behind the frustration, behind the injustices, behind the inhumanities, behind every oppression, there is a spiritual power. At bottom, we have been liberated from it. But not yet in actuality. So, let us understand the situation well. The demons are still around; they lurk behind human injustice, deceit, cruelty, greed, apathy. We have a real fight on our hands, but it is the kind of fight the church can wage.

Need we ever wonder why things never go wholly right in the world? Why do our dreams never fully come true? Why do the best laid plans for wars on poverty get bogged down in human inertia or political ineptitude, to say nothing of knavery? Why do the most cultured of peoples let themselves be led into a madman's war of conquest? Why are national aspirations never satisfied without bloodletting? Why are things never in control? Why? Things are not what they seem. There are powers beyond our control, forces that we cannot defeat by our human weapons. There are powers that it took the Son of God to come to grips with. "The Son of God appeared for the very purpose of undoing the devil's work."[2] And in His strength, we move out in strength.

* * *

The church does not have to have all the answers. Few preachers are experts on a just tax system. The church

[1] Ephesians 6:12   [2] I John 3:8

need not know when and how to trade in what goods with China. The church does not have expertise on welfare spending, on urban recovery, or on environmental cleansing. It is not a bureau of technicians. It cannot open its mouth on every problem in society. But it can pronounce judgment on the unjust, indifferent, and cruel. It can demand justice; it can plead for the oppressed; it can open its hands to the poor. And it can speak of the victory of Christ over the powers that afflict the world with misery.

The church knows that it will not create God's Kingdom on earth; only God can bring in the new creation. It knows that it will not establish a perfect world that will make God's final coming superfluous. It knows its limits. But it also knows that it ought to do what its hands find to do in Christ's name, for "in the Lord its labor will not be lost."[1]

[1] I Corinthians 15:58